THE
MIRROR

7 Steps to
REFLECT The Life You Want™

Tim Howard & Maria Spears

Cover and interior design by BookBaby Publishing.

Print ISBN: 978-1-66786-124-1
eBook ISBN: 978-1-66786-125-8

"Life is an echo. What you send out comes back. What you sow, you reap. What you give, you get. What you see in others, exists in you."

— ZIG ZIGLAR

Dedication

To Conner, Cole and Clayton

Follow your dreams!

To Matt

My "Gift from God"

May we always 'REFLECT'

Christ to one another.

CONTENTS

FOREWORD

We become on the outside what we believe on the inside, because our beliefs determine our expectations and have the power to influence everything we do now, and our experiences in the future.

Years ago, when I began my pursuit of self-discovery, I came across a quote that read:

> "If you bring forth what is within you,
> what you bring forth will save you.
> If you do not bring forth what is within you,
> what you don't bring forth will destroy you."

The catalyst for me was making a shift in my profession as a practicing Registered Nurse to working in the direct sales industry from home while growing my family. I had no idea at the time how I would be required to change so that I could change my life. Navigating the transition proved challenging for many reasons. I did not have prior experience in sales, nor did I know how to run a business much less grow a team or understand how to develop others into leaders. In fact, what I realized was that while I understood my passion of serving others, and the fulfillment that gave me to be able to make a positive impact in and on the lives of others. I would not grow beyond a certain point in my business until I grew personally.

It's been said that the greatest obstacle of discovery is not ignorance, but the illusion of knowledge. Through the years I have found that I needed to shift my own perspective and the illusion of knowledge in order to improve, grow, and ultimately enlarge others, and not just be "open to change" but to "pursue change".

If this is something that you also desire for yourself and in your life try focusing your energy on that of which you desire to become. Out of the many resources that have helped me through the years, including the lessons gained through my own experiences.

I had had a breakthrough on what had become the illusion of knowledge for me. I had gone to work on shifting my perception on how I viewed the experience. However, the experiences were now patterns repeating themselves because I had not shifted my belief within myself that I had the power to change the actual experiences over just changing my mindset around the experience.

Which is why I feel compelled to share the value of "The Mirror", co-authored by my friends Tim Howard and Maria Spears. Throughout the book they share concepts, now the title of a podcast, "REFLECT The Life You Want™", and personal stories, neuroscience, practical exercises, and techniques to break through limiting beliefs, strategies on mind management and understanding of the power of our thoughts.

Following the steps of the acrostic R.E.F.L.E.C.T. will lead you to a life of greatness. It embodies every element needed to bridge the gap of who you are now to that of which you desire to become.

I am blessed to have found their friendship and mentorship because it leads to life changing solutions and the perfect framework in being able to create the life of my dreams, including the one component I had simply overlooked unknowingly in the process, were R and E of their acrostic REFLECT.

* Don't change just enough to get away from your problems— change enough to solve them.

* Don't change your circumstances to improve your life— change yourself to improve your circumstances.

* Don't wait to see the light in order to change — start changing as soon as you feel the heat.

* Don't see change as something hurtful that can't be done — see it as something helpful that can be done.

* Don't avoid the immediate price of change — if you do you will pay the ultimate price of never improving."

Your willingness to take a deep dive and embark on a journey of self-discovery in order to live a life you desire is the first step to an ongoing journey. However, being able to find the right roadmap is key to your success.

As you read this book and begin to apply their strategies in your life you will find that despite your circumstances and experiences that you have the power to change your life and will have everything you need to bring forth what is within you and create the life of your dreams. The ripple effect it will extend beyond you into the lives around you by mirroring your own reflection, will in turn light the path of darkness for others.

Heather Clark
Green Compass™

PREFACE

TIM

The concept of *The Mirror* first came to me while completing a Master's Program when I worked for a Fortune 100 company. I was selected as part of a small group of up-and-coming leaders to participate in a two-year corporate leadership program. In the first year, the program focused on gaining a deep understanding of self in order to develop greater emotional intelligence. The second year capitalized on these insights to develop enhanced leadership skills, for significant organizational change, and improved business results. The company's investment in my learning enabled me to lead changes that resulted in tens of millions of dollars of improved, sustained business results not only for my employer, but subsequent organizations as well.

It was during this training that I was introduced to the foundational communication model called "The Interpersonal Gap," developed by John Wallen. We applied what we learned of this model through experiential skill groups, which enabled us to begin to recognize that our judgments—our thoughts, feelings, and actions about others—are "ours"—and therefore can be changed.

However, this is a skill developed over time. The process of un-learning established behaviors involves rewiring our brains to new ways of thinking and new behavioral skills in order to communicate more effectively. Nevertheless, it is a set of skills that will serve us more effectively in life as we journey forward.

Whether you agree with me right now or not, I ask you to suspend your judgment and open your mind to the possibility of new ways of thinking as you read this book. Improving your communications skills will help close the gap and enhance all the relationships in your life, both personally and professionally.

MARIA

I would like to present a caveat to the scientific research we share throughout this book. One of the things Tim and I have learned in this growth journey is just how quickly scientific understanding of the body and brain is changing. On top of that when it comes to various concepts we share with you and things we've learned, even those may have changed by the time you are reading this. The amazing thing about growth is it never ends.

To this point, Tim and I have shared what we've learned, what has been beneficial to us and what we believe to be beneficial to you, but that being said, by the time you are reading this, some (or much!) of the science and/or concepts could have changed. So take what's helpful and ditch what's not!

INTRODUCTION

TIM

I've been on a journey. For the past fifteen years. I've been on a journey to discover a deeper meaning and purpose in life, which has evolved as this book project has progressed. Many of the things I've learned along the way are laid out in the pages of this book.

At times, this book project was on the back burner. At other times, it was in the forefront of my mind, awaiting the right person to come alongside me to write the "other view." I needed the right collaborator to help me flesh out and challenge my ideas, bring their own ideas, and help the story come to life on these pages.

I'm grateful that I was introduced to Maria, who has met those needs perfectly.

Our intention is that you apply the principles we share in order to transform your thinking and discover your own unique calling and purpose. You are created for greatness, for wholeness, for completeness. You are designed to grow into your calling and step fully into your abilities.

This book will help you to REFLECT The Life You Want™!

MARIA

Do you feel stuck in your life? Do you believe that you are forever defined by your past? What would it be like to know and believe where you are right now doesn't have to be your future? The truth is that your past doesn't have to be a stop sign; it can actually be the dynamite to propel you to an incredible future.

Perhaps you have wondered why some people always seem so happy and things always seem to go their way, while you seem to have a black cloud always hanging over you. What if I told you there is a secret sauce for having joy and happiness in your life and the "black cloud" can be lifted if you just choose to make a few shifts?

I want you to know and believe in your heart and mind that you can have a good future and be filled with hope. Each of us has a God-given super power, but many of us have never been shown how to use it. (Hint: you do...and you'll learn more about it as you read this book!)

I am so excited for you to open these pages and journey with us. It's a journey I started years ago that culminated as I learned through reading and studying and prayer and practice just how much power God has given us and the gift of our Free Will. He has literally given us the tools to live a life of abundance: "I have come that they may have life and have it in abundance!"[1]

I'm not saying life will always be daisies and rainbows. But what I am saying is that all of us have some tools in our toolbox that most people either aren't aware of or don't know how to use.

You, too, have these tools; you've always had them. But no one has taken the time to show you how to use them so you can live with more freedom, joy, transformation and love … until now.

Dear reader, I invite you to journey with us and keep an open heart and an open mind. Enter into this period of discovery wholeheartedly, with humility, and really give it a go. Give yourself permission to dream the "what ifs" … give yourself permission to explore and believe the possibilities and the impossibilities. God's dreams over you are so much greater than your own. Believe it.

Now, let's take that first step....

---

1. John 10:10

THE MIRROR

Recognize that you have the power to change your life.

Each day reflect on what you are grateful for already.

Feel the happiness now that you imagine it will be when…

Love yourself and let others know you love them.

Energize your thoughts towards what you intend to be.

Clarify your inner circle.

Thoughts are key. Think it—Create it!

REFLECT The Life You Want™

CHAPTER 1

"As water reflects the face, so one's life reflects the heart" —Proverbs 27:19

*"When we are no longer able to **change** a situation, we are challenged to **change** ourselves." —Viktor E. Frankl*

Recognize your power to change.

TIM'S VIEW

In the early days of writing this book, I came across the following:

"If you do not like the image in the mirror do not break the mirror, break your face" –Old Persian Proverb

I thought to myself, *how do I break my face?* Deciding to explore the point, I grabbed my *Roget's Thesaurus* off the shelf and discovered the very first synonym for "face" was "countenance."

Wow! That definitely correlated to the theme of this book. But did it apply to me personally? Standing in front of a mirror, I took a good look at my countenance.

My hair is prematurely salt-and-pepper gray. My eyebrows encroach over my eyes slightly. My chin has more flesh below it than I'd care to see. And then I noticed the sides of my mouth are generally turned down.

Curious if I'd always had the same downturned appearance, I went in search of some old pictures of myself as a child. I pulled out the old metal filing box my mom got for me when I was a child and began to sort through the memorabilia.

I was all smiles in the kindergarten class photo. The same was true from first thru sixth grade. A different look, however, appeared in seventh grade —the toothy smile was replaced by a smile of only slightly upturned lips. My eighth grade picture was missing, but there was a photo of me pinning an opponent on the wrestling mat, all smiles. No smile in ninth grade at all. A slight smile in tenth and eleventh led up to a big, healthy grin for the senior photo.

When you know someone is taking your picture, you are more apt to "smile for the camera." The real test is in the impromptu moments. What was my prevailing disposition? What thoughts in my mind were manifesting in my emotions and physical appearance?

I suddenly realized that somewhere along the way my countenance *had* changed. My downturned appearance was the first impression I was now giving to most people and decided I'd rather greet others with a happy countenance.

This was an opportunity for me to "break my face."

It brought to mind what a former work associate once said: "It takes only seventeen muscles to smile versus forty-three to frown." I don't know if science supports this or not, but the principle remains that it doesn't take a lot of effort to smile.

I decided to change.

How I "Broke" My Face

Recently I had a couple of headshots taken for my real estate business at an annual meeting event. My team administrator sent me an unsolicited message that she thought I looked really happy and inviting in the photos. I was struck by that. My efforts to change were paying off.

What were the things that happened to bring this about? How was I clearly exuding more joy and happiness than before?

It wasn't because my life had suddenly become easy and perfect. In fact, in the ten years it has taken me to write this book, I have experienced some of the most challenging situations of my life. There have been lots of personal and professional changes; some made by me and some made for me. All had consequences that affected my psyche and how I showed up in the world. Yet somewhere along the way, when I started to get better control of my thinking and mindset, I experienced incredible growth spiritually, physically, emotionally, economically. My health improved. Joy returned.

I can take no credit for at all for my spiritual growth. God chose to remove something from my life that was holding me back from being the best version of myself. The others came about through my focused efforts to improve my life. Intentionality and consistency have been the keys.

Taking action to carry out decisions yields positive results. It isn't rocket science. Moving forward requires determination and diligence when developing new, healthier habits. You must recognize the need within you for change and then set about making changes to achieve your specific goals. Seek new challenges in the uncharted areas of your life.

> **Sometimes when we are at our worst,**
> **we make the decisions that propel us to become our best.**

When I look at some of the most successful people in business or the most spirit-filled in their faith, there is often the common theme of remarkable change following incredible hardship or tragedy. Sometimes when we are at our worst, we make the decisions that propel us to become our best.

Yet we don't have to wait until the pain of remaining the same outweighs the pain of change for change to occur. We each are in total control of one thing: our minds.

Don't buy into the belief that someone can make you feel or think something. They can't make you change your opinion of yourself, at least not without your permission. Yes, their words can be hurtful, but nobody gets to define who you are, other than God. And for Him, your identity arises out of His unconditional love for you.

The Importance of Mindset

We are constantly faced with choices about what to do with our thoughts and emotions:

- How do I convey my ideas in a way that they are understood?
- How can I be truly heard?
- How do I let others know how they're impacting me?
- Why do I feel the need to convince you that "I'm right?"
- How do I replace negative, toxic thoughts about myself with healthier ones?
- How do I impart positive thinking to others?

Our minds process thousands of bits of data every second based on what we hear, see, think, and feel. Yet we can only contemplate four to seven thoughts at a time and we can only focus on a single task. Multi-tasking is a myth. When people say that, they are just shifting their focus from one item to the next.

Each thought is evaluated and judged in our brain. It's happening right now as you read these words. Such a continuous onslaught can lead to problems, which is why sleep and our Reticular Activating System (RAS) are so important. The RAS is a diffuse network of nerve pathways in the brainstem connecting the spinal cord, cerebrum, and cerebellum, and mediating the overall level of consciousness. It is constantly processing information for us and helps to keep us safe.

Past Experiences, Present Perspectives

Much of the evaluation is taking place on an almost unconscious level. We are filtering the data through a frame of reference based on our life experiences. Our thoughts are shaded by our beliefs that are formed over time, much of it at an early stage in our lives.

It is said that much of our personalities are essentially determined by age seven. Our family of origin is a powerful system that affects our outlook on life until we realize it does not have to truly determine our reactions. The patterns of thought and beliefs that we have formed can be changed. It takes work. It takes having an intellectual curiosity to be open to the possibility of new ideas. It takes a willingness to break down old ideas, old patterns of behavior, and form new ways of thinking, which leads to new actions and new outcomes.

Consider my story. I held an irrational fear of doctors and hospitals for many years as an adult. When I finally took time to analyze it, I realized my fear was fueled by my childhood medical experiences. Subconsciously, a movie reel of past events played in my mind every time I walked into a medical facility:

I'm one year old, lying in a hospital bed recovering from surgery. There is a television mounted to the wall or ceiling, up high. I'm too young to make sense of it. I'm awake, then asleep.

I'm six years old, standing on the steel frame of a chair in my bedroom closet trying to reach a game on the top shelf. My foot slips and I fall to the floor, hitting my chin on the corner of the chair, causing a huge gash. I'm screaming, crying, blood is everywhere. Mom runs into my room, then I'm at the doctor's office. I feel the pain of the needle as they inject it into my chin to "numb" the pain before they patch me up. Oh, the irony.

Then we were headed from the pediatricians office to the university hospital downtown for further evaluation for whether I'd need 'plastic surgery'.

Thirteen stitches later, an additional consultation, I'm riding in the car, headed home. An eighteen-wheeler jackknifes in front of us, whipping back and forth across multiple lanes of freeway before bouncing off the railing and coming to a stop. Unhurt, Mom and I sit in the car, trying to calm down after the two terrifying events of the day.

I'm sixteen years old. I'm driving a Kelly-green Datsun 510 wagon to the Friday night football game between my high school and our crosstown rivals. My brother, Vince, is in the passenger seat, with the seat tilted back. It's dusk and I don't see the oncoming car, so I begin to turn left.

Crash. We hit head on. Vince flies headfirst into the windshield. My knees slam into the dashboard below the steering wheel. Our car rolls over and lands on the driver's side door.

Vince is now at my feet. There's blood everywhere. Someone helps me out of the car. I'm crying, "Someone please help my brother!" The firemen take the windshield off the car to get Vince out. He lets out a blood-curdling scream as he regains consciousness when they move him to get him out of the car. I'm terrified.

My mom and dad were at a local shopping mall when they were paged to be notified of what had happened. Mom later says she knew we were going to be alright. She is a woman of strong religious faith. My dad was apparently less assured. My brother lives.

These are just a few of the thousands of life experiences that shape my outlook today. The scar on my abdomen, the scar on my chin, the memory of a scream. These are some of the more vivid memories that can be triggered by words or an image that I encounter during the day.

There are literally hundreds of memories that shape our perceptions each day. These memories form the reflection of a two-way mirror through which we see our lives. Filtering our perspective on every thought, every feeling, and every conversation we have.

Your power is in the present.

Past is past, present is now. The future will be determined by the thoughts and feelings you are creating right now. Your power is in the present. You cannot change the past, but you can reframe how you think about it. The future has not yet happened, but you have the power to change it by reshaping your thoughts right now.

What thoughts are you currently holding on to that do not serve you now? You can let go of them. I know you can because I did.

Letting Go of Fear

While writing this book and working on my mindset, I was suddenly faced with my childhood fears all over again.

It was the Sunday after Thanksgiving. My wife, three teenage boys, and I were on our way home to Wilmington, North Carolina from New Orleans when we stopped in Montgomery, Alabama for lunch. After a quick browse through a guitar shop near the restaurant, we headed back to the minivan to resume the long drive home.

My oldest son was standing behind his mom as she opened the driver's door, the corner of which hit him right above his left eye and cut him deeply. After handing him my red bandana handkerchief to apply pressure to the cut, I ran back into the restaurant to get directions to the nearest hospital.

My fears of going to the doctor/hospital were right before me.

Not wanting to pass my fear off to my son, I began to think about how I was responding in the moment. As my fifteen-year-old experienced his first emergency room trauma, I focused on remaining calm and reassuring.

I watched as they administered a local anesthetic. Why is it that the treatment is always seems to be more painful than the injury?

I was proud of him as he endured the pain bravely, not even complaining. After the physician left, I began to clean him up, gently washing away all the blood on his forehead, his neck, and in his hair as I reassured him that it was going to heal up quickly, how the stitches would disappear, how he'd likely have a cool scar. It was my way of wiping away the pain so he would not develop the irrational fears I had as a boy.

By the time he was released, he was cracking jokes and letting his mom know that he was okay. It's interesting how an experience that I once feared is now laughed about amongst our family.

To this day, my son always carries a red bandana-style handkerchief with him. I'm not quite sure of the significance for him, but I hope it symbolizes how his dad was with him that day in the hospital, showing him love and reassuring him that all was going to be okay. Kind of like our Heavenly Father.

His experience was a turning moment for me. It allowed me to recognize that I no longer have to think and feel as I did when I was six years old; I don't have to be afraid anymore. Since I've learned that my thoughts control my emotions and how I respond to such circumstances, I now choose to focus on positive things, such as gratitude for the trained professionals who provide care for me and my family and other families every day.

By the time the next medical emergency arose in my family, it was evident that my efforts to overcome my fears were working. While at a friend's house, my youngest son fell off a golf cart and broke both bones in his left arm, just below the wrist. Upon receiving the call from the friend's mother and learning that she was taking him to the hospital, I calmly said, "Okay," hung up the phone, and told my wife. I suddenly remembered the lesson I'd learned as a young Lieutenant in the Army: People will follow you when you can remain calm and assured in tense situations.

I realized yet again that I have total power over how I respond to an emergency. Yes, instincts will kick in when I need them to, but I am responsible for my outlook, and I choose to not be afraid.

Many of us struggle to control what happens in our lives. Control needs are usually based upon some sort of fear from past experiences. What if you could shift the focus within yourself from a fear-based desire for control to a joyous expectancy for what you want and desire? You can. You will.

What Do You See in the Mirror?

Maybe you see only what you want to see. Or maybe you're willing to see the reflection of who you truly are. Maybe you can identify things about yourself that you want to keep, as well as things you'd like to change.

Whether you realize it or not, you are reflecting your true image to others all day long. For good or for bad, you bring your whole-life experience with you each day. Will you allow the past to continue to determine your future by focusing only on where you've been? Will you continue to be frustrated with where you are? Or will you start to see the life you want and create it—beginning right now?

The things we bring with us from the past affect every aspect of our lives: our relationships, our work, our parenting, and so forth. Hopefully, most of our memories are good ones but I'm sure there are some experiences we would rather forget, especially for those of us who were victims of some sort of abuse.

As you begin to reflect on your past, not only will you gain a greater insight regarding the images you see of yourself, you will also gain a greater insight into the image you are projecting onto others.

You may have some work to do. Like I was, are you holding on to fears that you need to let go? Are you carrying resentment towards someone? Do you need to forgive someone? Do you need to forgive yourself?

Each of us has developed our own set of behaviors that we use to cope in our daily lives. Some of these behaviors serve us well, some not so well.

Our relationships are central to our being. We were created to be in relationship with one another. Yes, we have our sense of self and our own lives, but life would be pretty empty without friends and those we love. Communication is key to any relationship. Understanding how we communicate and why we project what we do, will enable us to improve and enrich the relationships we have with others.

Communication—A Reflective Model

What if you realized that every relationship you have and every interaction with every person is a reflection of your own thoughts and feelings about yourself? Would this cause you to change how you looked at others? Would you want to reconsider what you attract into your life?

Our "encoding" and "decoding" can be thought of as "filters." These show up in our thoughts as words like "should" in our judgments, which are based on our beliefs. I came to understand that much of my belief system originated in my family of origin. How I related to authority figures or leaders I worked for had to do with the leadership exhibited in my family growing up. How I related to peers had a lot to do with how I related to siblings or other children during my childhood. The norms I developed while growing up became the tapes I played in my mind as I related to others as an adult.

During my second year of my Master's program where I was introduced to the "Interpersonal Gap" method, I had a personal breakthrough. So much of what I had focused on in skill groups was trying to interpret the intention of others but all of a sudden, a light bulb went on, allowing me to see myself by my interpretation of others. My judgments were more a reflection of me than the other person or the situation.

Slowly I began to recognize that when I made judgment calls, I needed to stop and ask myself—is this about me? I found that at least half the time the judgment had more to do with me than the other person or the situation. For example, when I didn't like the actions or the behavior of another person, I would remember times in the past when I had behaved in a similar way … or failed to act at all.

This was enlightening. I find that most people would complete this statement "I know you by your … actions." Where in reality, it's "I know you by my interpretation of your actions." When I recognized this,

- the focus of my attention began to be self-reflective and introspective rather than reactionary,
- the capacity to withhold my judgments increased, and
- my ability to respond from a clear sense of myself began to grow.

Here is a look at the "Interpersonal Gap" model:

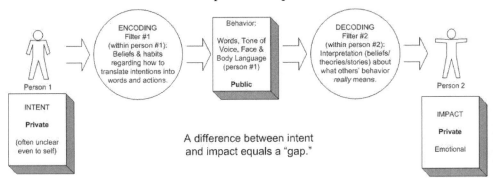

When I share The Interpersonal Gap model with others now, I add a "mirror" on the left-hand side, between "intent" and "encoding." Another "mirror" could also be added to the right-hand side between "decoding" and "impact." I believe that the majority of the judgments we make about others or circumstances are actually a reflection of ourselves. The key skill is to learn not to immediately react to a circumstance, but rather take in what is heard or seen and analyze the situation first. Is this something that is relevant to you? Is this something that you want to know more about? Is this something you want to explore? Or is this just information that is neutral to you?

Oftentimes, the things that resonate most with me are things that I either:

1. like about myself or aspire to be more like, or

2. things I tend to criticize about myself.

It is critical to capture our thoughts and decide what is let in, thereby guarding our hearts. On the one hand, we don't need to take on other people's drama or judgments. On the other hand, we may need to allow compliments and encouragement to fill our hearts. We were designed in the image of God, to love and to be loved. We need connections with others, especially when they are life affirming.

It is my belief that our identity is not about what other people think of us; there is only one judge I ultimately concern myself with. We do need to be mindful, however, of the impact we are making on others and how effective we are in communicating with each other. Is our life exhibiting the values and ideals we desire? Are we leaving a positive impact on others from our interactions with them? We can't "make" anybody feel anything, but our words and actions certainly can trigger either powerfully positive or negative reactions. You can choose to leave a positive impact on others.

The mirror is a powerful awakening to self-awareness and sensitivity to others that requires a level of intentionality and focus during interactions. It requires your presence and an awareness of when the clarity of the mirror becomes foggy or highly distorted.

The thoughts we allow to enter our mind have consequences—for good or for bad. They pass through our filters and take up physical real estate within our neurological wiring. The great thing is, we are capable of performing our own "brain surgery" by rewiring our thoughts. We can choose to shift our perspectives and form new neurological pathways with healthier thinking habits.

It is helpful to focus on being a clear mirror. Ideally, to see the best in others, it's helpful to reflect the best of ourselves.

Pursue Your Dreams

There is a lot of power in dreaming. It unlocks within each of us our deepest desires and the importance of pursuing our purpose in life. As we work on chasing our dreams, we're able to become the best version of ourselves—our highest selves.

One of the original meanings of the word "Desire" is the Latin phrase, "de sire" or "of the Father." Napoleon Hill says desire is "the first step towards achievement."[2] Therefore, desire is the motivation to achieve our dreams and live out the purpose for our lives. We are intended to live a fulfilling life. I wouldn't have the desire in my heart if God did not give me the ability to achieve it. It is my gift to the world.

Mature desires are those that make our hearts sing! It is important to work on clarifying within yourself, in your mind and in your heart, what things

---

2. Napoleon Hill, *Think and Grow Rich*

make your heart sing. A print that hangs in my office reads, "Be fearless in the pursuit of what sets your soul on fire!" Those dreams are worth pursuing.

Success is not by luck, but by law; there is a science to our success. The natural laws of the universe give us precise directions about how we should pursue our dreams. Not in a 'woo-woo' way, but in the sense that God made the universe to operate within a certain set of principles and in understanding those principles it can be a powerful recipe for success. For our goal setting, it is recommended that we go after our impossible dreams—ones that scare us yet excite us at the same time. As Walt Disney reportedly said, "To succeed, [you must] work hard, never give up, and above all cherish a magnificent obsession."

We need to learn to cultivate our desires—those things that resonate with us and excite us—by paying attention to what keeps coming to mind again and again. Our desires will reveal our calling, our contribution. Our desires will mature as we grow. As Saint Catherine of Siena is credited with saying, "Be who God meant you to be and you will set the world on fire."

When we are living on purpose, we are living our best with the least amount of effort. We are focused, we are disciplined, we live consistently, we have joy, and we experience freedom in our calling. The greatest reward in achieving our dreams is our contribution to who we become! We need to take action in faith –in God, ourselves and the people who walk with us. We need to be intentional about chasing the dreams that will lead us to our unique calling. We want to connect with these desires in order to begin to create, and then bring forth our contribution. "Chase *you*!"

There can be roadblocks that are holding us back (e.g., a concern about having a bad reputation or misinformation from others in our lives). We need to neurologically rewire our thinking to let go of self-limiting beliefs and unleash our full potential. Let's master our mindset skills and become the best version of ourselves. It's time for transformation!

Are you satisfied with where you are in life? Are you content with who you've become? If not, you have the power to change your circumstances—and you will, when you realize that you can. You will when you believe in yourself, realize that your thoughts and feelings are yours and yours alone, and that you can control or change them.

Your future is bright. Look in the mirror. Start seeing yourself as the person you want to become. Smile and realize that it is within you. *Right now!*

MARIA'S VIEW

Have you ever seen yourself a certain way and locked into that label? Maybe you were the star athlete in high school and college and still hold on to that badge of honor. Maybe you were the cheerleader now turned CEO of a company and you are holding on to the label that you're the woman who has it all together.

The problem with labels is that too often they become safety nets. We can be so busy protecting that "old wiring" and belief of who we are that we miss even greater opportunities of becoming a better, more authentic version of who we are created to be.

Music was my safety net. I had always been the musician. I started playing and singing in public when I was ten years old and haven't stopped since. My teen years were spent playing for so many youth events, or retreats, or conferences, or other random gigs. Everyone knew me as the musician. I kept that title and earned it even more in college. After college I continued to play and sing and travel the world; broadening my music repertoire to everything from Christian music to country, rock, jazz or even classical. Wherever I was, I was associated with music. I didn't realize how wrapped up my identity was as a musician until it was unexpectedly placed on hold.

New Identity—New Opportunities

I'll always remember that night. A million thoughts ran through my mind as I sat in my car in front of the Krav Maga and Brazilian Jiu Jitsu studio and debated whether to go in and train, or go home and take a run instead. My grandma had died the day before and to say I wasn't in the best head or heart space to train was an understatement.

Against my better judgment and gut intuition, I went inside, changed into my uniform, and stepped onto the mat. Thirty minutes later, my life and perspective was changed forever.

Anyone who has trained in martial arts knows the importance of being fully present mentally and emotionally. Try as I might, my thoughts were everywhere except where they should have been: On the sensei who was giving instructions and demonstrations for hip throws.

As soon as the guy I had "hip thrown" landed on my foot, I lost my balance. Hearing a "pop" and feeling a searing pain in my knee, I knew it wasn't good. I tried to shake it off but I couldn't put weight on it and I felt as though I would pass out. As the pain got worse, I breathed slowly, intentionally, forcing myself to be calm. *I will be okay*, I told myself. *It's just a strain. I'll be back up and ready to test for my belt in a few weeks as planned.*

But my mindset didn't match my reality. The MRI showed I had shredded my ACL, MCL, and Meniscus. Surgery was going to be necessary, the doctors said, if I wanted to get back to my usual level of fitness and activity. I was devastated. As a traveling musician and a personal trainer, everything I did required me to be active. Not only that, if I couldn't do any of my normal activities, who would I be?

All kinds of questions started to run through my head during my recovery: Who am I if I'm done playing music and performing? Who am I if people don't know me as the girl who is on stage singing and playing? Do people love me for me, for myself, or simply for what I bring to the music table? Do I have worth outside of being a musician? Lord, why did you let this happen?

The next six to twelve months was a journey … a journey of letting go of who I was in order to open myself up to the woman I was to become. The woman God created me to be. The woman I *wanted* to be, but hadn't known how.

It was a humbling experience. I was always the person taking care of everyone else and suddenly I was the one needing help. I couldn't even go to the bathroom or shower by myself.

I felt like I had regressed back to being a young child again where my sweet mom had to help me with those basic human necessities.

There is a certain humility that helplessness creates; and looking back on that time I am so grateful for the ways my amazing parents and roommate cared for me at different points and in different ways.

When I could finally drive again (using my left leg to push the gas and brake; don't tell the cops!), I left Kentucky where my parents were taking care of me and drove back to Tennessee. When I got to my apartment, I realized that both of my roommates were gone for several days. After many failed attempts to carry my suitcase inside, I climbed back in my car and cried before calling a friend who drove twenty minutes to come help. I was mortified, and yet this friend was so precious and gracious and more than happy to serve.

Yet the injury that was such a devastation was also necessary to bring forth a massive blessing. This experience taught me the importance and beauty of receiving. We can't be good givers until we are also good receivers. When we act strong and are always the givers, we withhold the opportunity for others to love on us, to serve us, which is also a gift to *them*.

We can't be good givers until we are also good receivers.

What I Desire Most I Push Away

Have you ever deeply desired something, yet you found yourself pushing it away and self-sabotaging instead?

While attending a small, private Catholic university in Ohio, I became friends with one of the girls in my "Household" (similar to a sorority but meant to be a sisterhood to build each other up, grow in faith and service, etc.). Every time I saw her on campus, I gave her a hug (I'm Italian after all, we hug everyone!) even though I felt her tense up a little, making it seem as though maybe she didn't appreciate it.

During one of our meetings our senior year, we went around and shared positive things that stood out to us about each other during our time together at the school. When my friend came to me, tears spilled down her cheeks. "You may have noticed I don't initiate much in the way of physical touch with anyone," she said. "But you always went out of your way to hug and appreciate me even though I responded awkwardly. I want you to know how much that meant to me. You see, at home growing up, there wasn't a lot of hugging or physical touch. It's what I crave the most and yet I have no idea how to respond to it. But it is how I feel most loved. Thank you."

Perhaps you can relate. I know I can.

When I first moved to Nashville, many people assumed it was for music. It was in fact, the opposite. After traveling so much for music, mission work, and fun (I managed to scratch off some bucket-list items!), I needed a break. I sought a hiatus from the hectic pace and desired more of a "normal" life. You know, where I'm actually in town sleeping in my own bed, in my own house on the weekend.

Ironically, the first few years were really hard. Living a more "like everyone else" life was a massive shift for a girl who was used to being everywhere except in one place. This shift also caused me to reconsider my gifts and talents.

As my music hiatus dragged on longer than planned, I started to think that season of my life was actually over. Looking back, I can see how taking that break from music and reorienting myself was important. Yet living in Nashville put me in the continual presence of incredible musicians, causing the comparison game to regularly play in my head.

It's been said that "comparison is the thief of joy." I can definitely attest to that statement. I would even add that when you let it continue, it can lead to depression. Add comparison to a devastating moment in life and it can be a recipe for a sad life.

My boyfriend and I had just broken up and not a month later, my music teacher, who was a dear friend, was murdered. A slew of more painful life events followed. To say that I was in a rough head and heart space is an understatement.

However, even in our painful moments, God sends us life rafts. For me, He sent Christine and Kara (or "Chris" and "Kare" for short) who became two of my best friends and housemates. We had a unique sisterhood and friendship that can only be described as a sheer gift from God.

While in Kansas City with Chris and Kare for an event that I didn't particularly want to be at because of how sad and depressed I was, I "randomly" ran into an old friend of mine—a fellow musician whom I hadn't seen in years. (I put "randomly" within quotation marks because at this time in my life I am firmly convinced nothing is coincidental. *Nothing* just happens by happenstance. Everything is actually orchestrated to bring about a greater good by a Father who works in the intricate details of our lives.)

"Maria!" he exclaimed. "So good to see you; how are you? Are you still playing music all over?"

"Actually, no," I responded. "I took a break when I moved to Nashville and just haven't gotten back into it."

"*Why*?" His voice held a level of shock and seriousness that surprised me.

"Well…." I paused to think for a second. Why *wasn't* I playing anymore? What was stopping me? Sure, two really serious, sad things had happened, but it used to be that I would play more when sad things happened. What was stopping me?

In a moment of extreme honesty, I said, "You know, I guess the truth is that I feel like it's not a big deal whether or not I play and sing." I rationalized how there were already so many incredible musicians, keys players, and vocalists on the scene who were significantly better than I was, that it didn't really matter if I played. I explained how music would always be a part of my life, but it would probably be limited to my living room. Yet even as I said these words, tears welled up in my eyes and a lump materialized in my throat.

He looked dumbfounded. Shaking his head and placing a hand on my shoulder, he said, "Maria, you have a gift to offer that *no one else can*! It doesn't matter if someone else plays and sings. It doesn't even matter if they play and sing the same songs or at the same events. You have a gift to offer in who you are. Your interpretation of the music is unique to you. Your talents were specifically given to you to bring light to the world in a way that no one else can. Don't ever stop playing."

Whoa. His words pierced me and have stayed with me. Soon after, Chris, Kare, and I began praying about starting a band and women's ministry.

Do you recognize that with the grace of God, you have the power to change your life? And that your life change can positively impact the lives of others? God has given you a free will, allowing your thoughts to massively impact you and your ability to make a difference in the world.

Compare and despair are two of the biggest obstacles blocking us from living a life of freedom and impact. Where is comparison preventing you from using your gifts?

> **Compare and despair are two of the biggest obstacles blocking us from living a life of freedom and impact.**

Something I have come to share regularly with the people I coach is that *each of us matters*. Our gifts matter. Who we are and how we show up matters. No one can replace you and no one can replace me. I remember reading some years ago that Scientists estimate the probability of your being born is somewhere around 1 in 400 *trillion*!!! Yes, you read that correctly; 1 in 400 *trillion*!!!

You and I are called, chosen, and have a specific mission from God. We aren't here just for ourselves; we're here to make a difference in the world and in people's lives and to become who He created us to be in the process. Our calling is to bring His Light to a dark world and cause ripple effects of His love. If you or I don't do it, no one can take that place. Each one of us is unique, individual and unrepeatable.

Through our individual gifts and talents, personalities, and life experiences, we are meant to touch specific people and to make a difference in our own unique way. It's that simple. You, your life, your calling: *you matter*.

"Before I formed you in the womb I knew you. Before
you were born I set you apart….." –Jeremiah 1:5

The Power of Hope

Do you struggle with hope?

I find that while many of us can lock in on the virtues of faith and love, many times hope seems to be elusive. Why is that? I believe it's because we look at our past and focus on the many disappointments. Maybe there have been a lot of beauty and good things as well, but often we only look back at what went wrong or not as we had planned.

Have you ever noticed how everything can be going great, when all of a sudden one sad or disappointing thing happens and the thing we focus on is that one negative instead of all the other amazing things?

Hope intimately ties in with our belief of who God is, whether or not He is actually a good Father. This doubt of the goodness of our Father goes all the way back to Genesis.

It was the serpent who put doubt in Eve's mind about God's goodness:

"Did He really say you couldn't eat from any tree in the garden?…. You won't die!" (Underlying message: God lies; He can't be trusted.)

"God knows if you eat from it your eyes will be open!" (Underlying message: God is holding back from you; He's not actually a good father!)

Now, that's me paraphrasing, but sowing seeds of doubt into who God is as Father—a *good* Father—severely dampens our ability to hope. How do you hope in someone who you don't trust is good, or wants your good? It's nearly impossible, I believe.

When I trust that I have a Father in heaven who is concerned about the details of my life and wants good for me, then I can approach life with an open heart, mind, and hands. I can go after my dreams without grasping, which puts me in a receptive state of abundance rather than scarcity. Hope has everything to do with abundance and being open to receiving the good and beautiful things our Father wants to give us!

But when we sow seeds of doubt about who our Father is, we in turn sow seeds of doubt into our identity as His children. Our perceived worth is diminished. Research has shown that we get our sense of who we are and our identity in a very real way from our earthly fathers. So if we don't know who our ultimate Father is, it makes it challenging to know who we are, which all ties into our worth and sense of self.

I have found one of the best practical ways to hold onto hope (besides prayer, of course!) is to dream. What would a beautiful life look like? Who would be in your life? Where would you live? What would you be doing? Whose lives would you be touching?

Creating that vision of a beautiful life and beautiful future also creates hope and anticipation of what could be. I remember reading that we are defined by memories of the past or a vision of the future. And it's true. We either go back into our memories of past experiences that we can't change, or we have the choice to look ahead at what could be.

Scripture says, "Without a vision, the people perish."[3] When we have a future and a belief that something beautiful *could* happen and *will* happen in our life, everything changes. It sparks a place in our hearts for excitement and anticipation and *hope*. That, in turn, also develops into faith and love. Scripture says to pray and then believe as though it has already happened.

> "Therefore I tell you, whatever you ask for in prayer, believe that you have received it, and it will be yours." –Mark 11:24

How many of us actually pray and believe like that? I know many times in the past, I haven't. But I'm starting to do it now! I pray for something and then, rather than going back and asking God for it again, I just start praising Him and thanking Him as though it has already happened!

---

3.   Proverbs 29:18.

- "Thank you Lord that you are taking care of so-and-so!"

- "Thank you Jesus that you are working all things for my good!"

- "Thank you Jesus that you have already answered this prayer and I'll get to see the fulfillment of it!"

Wow. There is *power* when we pray and hope like that.

I believe one of the biggest things holding us back these days is lack of hope. Hope that life can be better, hope that we can change, hope that our dreams and desires could actually come to be.

The enemy comes to steal, kill, and destroy.[4] One of the things he loves to destroy is our hope. Why? Because if we don't have hope, then we give up and we stop truly living because, well, what's the point? It doesn't matter anyway, right?

There is often a tension between where we are and where we desire to be. That "space between" is oftentimes a dance between hope and despair. How do you hold onto hope about something that you don't know will actually happen?

Ironically, if you let despair take over, then it will for sure not happen. Why? Because you will subconsciously self-sabotage it every time. If you don't actually believe something is going to happen (aka no hope!) then you're going to already feel disappointed. And if you're feeling disappointed, then you're not going to show up to your life in a way that would bring about those dreams or goals. Lack of hope and the emotions that follow don't lead to a life-giving result.

So what is the alternative? Step into believing it actually *could* happen! Why? Because if you believe it *could* happen, then you will view your life situations and circumstances differently. You will act in a way that can help create space and opportunities for those things to happen.

Living out of a place of hope is believing that what you desire *could* happen and that changes everything.

---

4. John 10:10

Maybe you're not in a place where you feel like you can hope fully yet, and that's okay. Maybe it's not that you don't want to hope, but your life experiences have "taught" you that hope leads to disappointment. I want you to consider the following:

- What if you could be wrong about that belief?
- What if the opposite could be true?
- What if there is a hope and a future for *you*?
- What if you let yourself practice the thought that a new future is possible?
- What would that change for you?

Now that you've heard all these stories, you may be wondering how they all connect. Through the lens of your life experience is the perspective you take on. It's through that perspective that you typically engage with people and the world.

I would venture to say that many of us are living out of a memory of the past and in many ways simply reliving it day after day. Why? Because at our core, while we may say we want to change, grow, heal, or have a different life, many of us don't know where to start. And if we are really honest with ourselves, we don't even believe it's possible. Without hope—without a vision—we perish. What we need is a new view. So let's see if we can gain a new perspective by coming from a place of HOPE:

Having an
Openness to what is
Possible and
Energizing.

It's important to identify who and where we are in life before launching into who and where we want to become.

Steps to Achieve Change

If anyone knows me, they know I am not one of those cold weather-loving kind of people. Ever since living in Ohio and experiencing the winters there, I've abhorred cold weather. I recently realized I had let my detest for it control a lot of my decisions. In fact, the more I thought *ugh, I hate the cold*, the worse it would be. After coming to that realization and seeing how my thoughts about the cold were limiting my life and getting in the way of some beautiful experiences, I decided it was time for a change.

First, I had to decide to shift my thinking. I couldn't simply say "I love the cold!" My brain instantly would have fired back to me, "No you don't! You hate it!" Because I had fostered an ingrained belief for so long, my brain and body assumed it to be true. So, ignoring my internal response, I decided to get curious.

I thought to myself, *Hmm, I wonder if I could enjoy the cold? A lot of people love the cold; I wonder what it is about it that they like? Could I become someone who enjoys it?* I began to consider what someone who enjoys the cold might think or feel when they are in a cold, snowy place. I thought, *Well, I bet they think it's beautiful.* So I booked a trip to Idaho to visit a dear friend and as I was driving the two hours from the airport to Sun Valley, I was blown away by the stark icy beauty.

It was so different from a drive through somewhere hot, like Arizona. But the sun still shone and the air was fresh. Before I knew it, I discovered one thing after another that I enjoyed about the cold, the snow, the ice, the wind.

I went skiing and although I didn't become an avid fan of the cold, I considered it to be really fun! I hiked with snowshoes and sat in hot springs in fifteen-degree weather with the stars twinkling above and freezing, rushing water around me. All of these things were delightful experiences that involved the *cold*!

What had actually changed? My *thoughts* about what I was looking for and what I was expecting!

When we expect to have a terrible time and be miserable, or that we won't like someone, we will almost always find that to be true. Our brain is always looking for proof to confirm our biases.

Knowing this, what kind of proof do you want to look for in your life? Do you want to see all the good, true, and beautiful things all around you? Do you want to see the gifts, miracles, and joys that happen every day? Or do you want to focus on all the bad, negative, and frustrating things? The choice is yours.

If you want to see the positive in life, consider what you want and start to look for proof—proof that there is goodness in the world, proof that God is good, and proof that life is a gift.

I promise you, if you look hard enough, you will begin to see it.

> **Our brain is always looking for proof**
> **to confirm our biases.**

The Science of Change

Every January 1, people set New Year's resolutions or goals, yet studies have shown that less than 25 percent of people keep their resolutions beyond 30 days, and only 8 percent accomplish them. Why? What's the problem?

We have this amazing computer system in our head called our brain and while it can help us accomplish anything and everything, it can also turn us into our own worst enemies.

Let's talk about it. Our brains have two main priorities: safety and efficiency. While these two priorities are necessary for survival, they aren't concerned with you living your best life.

These automatic and instinctual ways of thinking, feeling, and behaving are essentially habits that cause us to live our lives on autopilot; by default, if you will. *This* my friend, is why it's so challenging to change our behavior.

Setting goals isn't so difficult; the challenge lies in actually accomplishing them. To our brain, almost any change we try to make is perceived as a potential physical, mental, emotional, financial, and/or social risk.

Neuroscience has shown that the largest part of our brain (95-97 percent of it) functions in a deeper emotional and habitual way (subconsciously) while the smaller part of our brain (3-5 percent) operates logically and rationally (consciously).

Don't worry, we're not going to stay in the geeky brain science for too much longer, but it's important that you understand how to override what's going on in your mind so you can have hope that change is possible ... and actually make those changes!

Our subconscious brain is implicit, perceptual, habitual, and lightning fast. Our conscious brain is explicit, conceptual, deliberate, and super slow.

This explains why change can be so challenging: While we may set goals consciously, we typically operate out of our subconscious (i.e., our old beliefs, habits, and conditioning).

There is good news, though: *Change is possible* because of something called neuroplasticity.

Plasticity is the capacity to be molded, altered, or shaped. Thus, neuroplasticity is the ability for the brain to change or adapt over time by creating new neurons and building new networks in response to different life experiences.

Previously, scientists believed the brain stopped growing after childhood. This wouldn't necessarily be a bad thing if you had a great childhood with really positive brain wiring. But for most of us, if our brains were stuck with only learned behaviors from childhood, then we would be in some big trouble! We now know, however, that the brain is able to refine its architecture and/or shift functions to different regions of the brain throughout our lifespan.

Dr. Caroline Leaf, a communication pathologist and cognitive neuroscientist specializing in cognitive and metacognitive neuropsychology has said,

> "Our genetic makeup fluctuates by the minute based on what we are thinking and choosing... You control your genes; your genes do not control you. Genes may determine physical characteristics but not

psychological phenomena. On the contrary, our genes are constantly being remodeled in response to life experiences... Our choices become physiology, and what we believe as well as what we believe about ourselves alters the facts. We are not victims of our biology. We are co-creators of our destiny alongside God." (See 'Switch On Your Brain' by Dr. Caroline Leaf, p. 50-53)

In short, this means that it is possible to replace dysfunctional actions and patterns of thinking with new mindsets, skills, and abilities. Isn't that exciting?! You are *not* stuck and you are *not* a victim to your past or biology!

As Dr. Leaf stated, we are co-creators with God in many aspects of our lives. Isn't it amazing how much our God-given free will impacts our life–not just externally, but internally as well?

Applying Newton's First Law to Personal Change

Newton's first law states that every object will remain at rest or in uniform motion in a straight line unless compelled to change by the action of an external force. This is normally taken as the definition of inertia. The key point here is that if there is no net force acting on an object (if all the external forces cancel each other out) then the object will maintain a constant velocity. If that velocity is zero, then the object remains at rest. If an external force is applied, the velocity will change because of the force.

As human beings, we are highly resistant to change. Most people would rather succumb to the hardship of a poor life than endure the hardship of making a better one. The management training principle discussed previously in this book remains true in this context as well: Until the pain of remaining the same is greater than the pain of making the change, we will stay where we are. We need to have a compelling reason in our minds to make a change. We need to get in motion!

Every now and then, something external will cause a change in us—or at least our circumstances. But what I want us to focus on is a change in our mindset. We want to unlock our dreams and visualize a new version of ourselves.

We want to become the person we are called to be and elevate ourselves to our potential. The message here is: You *can* change your mindset and bring about the changes you want for yourself when you make the firm decision to do so.

We are in complete control of changing our mindset when we develop the skills of capturing our thoughts. We can replace thoughts that do not serve us with new and better thoughts.

Change requires making a decision. It's a decision no one else can make for you. "If it is to be, it is up to me."[5] Sustaining change requires us to develop new habits and daily routines. We also must focus on the compelling reason why we want or need to change. We can move from a mindset of "have to" to "get to." Because life happens for us, not to us.

Make the decision. Choose to move forward to live the life you want to create for yourself!

Life happens for us, not to us.

---

5.   -

JOURNAL EXERCISE

What thoughts are currently not serving you in your efforts to create the life that you want?

_____

_____

_____

_____

What thoughts would serve you in creating the life you want?

_____

_____

_____

_____

_____

What negative experiences can you reframe in your mind?

_____

_____

_____

_____

_____

Memorize and repeat the following "I AM a Thought Captor™!" affirmation:

> I am in control of my thoughts. I can change my thoughts. I can look at life differently. I can let go of thoughts that no longer serve me. I can take hold of thoughts that take me where I want.

Remember, developing an awareness of what we are thinking about is a vital skill. When a thought enters our mind that is not useful to us, that is not serving us, we must learn to recognize it, see what is underneath that thought and decide if we want to keep thinking it.

Contrary to what many of us think, we are not victims to our thoughts. We get to decide whether we let certain thoughts stay in our mind or not.

Do you actually believe your life can change? Why or why not? What would you want to change?

_____

_____

_____

_____

If you were going to change *one* thing in your life and focus on it for the next sixty to ninety days, what would it be? Why is this one thing so important to you? How would it impact your life and those around you if it did change?

Whatever that one thing is, write it down in present tense as though it has already happened and imagine what it would feel like:

- **I am so happy and grateful now that I am/have**….(a nonsmoker/ released ten pounds of weight/have a great relationship with my spouse/making "x" amount of money, etc.)
- **I/it feel(s)…**(so joyful/at peace/grateful/happy/amazing, etc.)

_____

_____

_____

_____

_____

CHAPTER 2

"Rejoice always, pray continually, give thanks in all circumstances; for this is God's will for you in Christ Jesus." —1 Thessalonians 5:16-18

"Gratitude is the healthiest of all human emotions. The more you express gratitude for what you have, the more likely you will have even more to express gratitude for." —Zig Ziglar

---

Each day reflect on what you are grateful for already.

TIM'S VIEW

I was headed down a path that seemed irreversible. I had made mistakes and those poor decisions now jeopardized not only my job, but my marriage and family as well—two things that I did not want to lose.

How had I gotten to that point? I had developed a lack of gratitude.

Instead of being content with what I had, I began to look elsewhere for things I didn't have. Rather than investing my time and energy at home, I spent it elsewhere. Were there areas in my marriage that needed to improve? Certainly. Relationships can always be improved. But I was focusing too much on what was wrong rather than embracing what was right. I was not making requisite deposits into the emotional bank accounts of my wife and sons.

By outward appearances, most people would think we had a good and happy marriage. But I was not happy.

I rationalized that my unhappiness was caused by others. When I looked in the mirror each day, I wanted more. That in and of itself was not the problem. The problem was that I hadn't been focusing on what needed changing—me.

So I started making some changes. As an outside observer you might think I was experiencing a midlife crisis. In a way, I guess I was. I set a goal to lose thirty pounds in eight weeks. It took me twelve, but I was getting back in shape and I felt great. I had more self-confidence, though I still lacked some of the self-esteem I thought I would gain from my physical transformation. I discovered it's not that simple.

Discovering Gaps

In my professional career, I was able to see the "gap" in a situation and determine how to fill it. As a problem solver, I helped organizations identify their weaknesses and develop strategies and tactics to improve their performance and grow their bottom lines. This was pretty typical in all my work environments: Work can be tough and stressful; a never-ending set of problems to fix and challenges to overcome.

After doing this for many years, I finally realized that I was only focusing on what was "wrong." I could see a problem quickly. I saw what was wrong before I saw what was right. I could read a financial statement or walk through a manufacturing operation and quickly identify things needing improvement.

Fortunately—or unfortunately—most of our weaknesses are overused strengths. Thus, I had the tendency to be critical. By setting high expectations and challenging people to meet them, I told myself that I was tough but fair. By not handing out much praise, I simply wasn't expecting anything more out of people than I would expect from myself. I used to tell myself that I was neither optimistic nor pessimistic—merely realistic.

But this approach doesn't won't work with a family. If you focus on what is wrong, you will be critical of the very ones who need your criticism the least:

your spouse, your children, your friends. They need your encouragement, love, support, and understanding. They need your gratitude; your acceptance.

Where does this outlook of seeing the gap come from? Look in the mirror. It comes from seeing the gaps we perceive in ourselves; all the "I should haves," "I wish I hadn't haves," "if only I would haves." Even though many of us have a very balanced and healthy emotional sense of well-being, we can be tough on ourselves sometimes. I heard it said recently that psychologists believe up to 85 percent of us came from what would be characterized as "dysfunctional" families. We've all got gaps, so we need to get over it!

Most of our weaknesses are overused strengths.

How did I change my perspective? I started focusing on what I appreciate about others—my wife, my children, my co-workers. It was hard at first since I was very attuned to the things that disappointed me, the things that annoyed me, the things that bothered me, the things that worried me. These were the things that readily came to mind throughout the day and as I tried to fall asleep at night.

Though I began thanking and encouraging others for their efforts and improvements, I quietly remained dissatisfied inside. Yes, the gaps got smaller as I applied strategies to improve the business problem, but the frustration didn't disappear.

There is a theory by Curt Lewin called "Force Field Analysis" that states when any change effort is begun, restraining forces always emerge. That's why it's important to listen to the objections and concerns of the "what about" and "it'll never work" naysayers. These concerns are valid; failing to address them is counterproductive. Remember, it is actually a compliment when an employee or friend or spouse raises these issues with you. It means they believe you have the power—or care enough—to do something about it.

In addition, what I've come to realize more recently is that what I focus on is what I create. If I am ungrateful, unappreciative, unloving, and unaware—this is what I get in return. You cannot avoid attracting what you think about; what you focus on expands. You cannot avoid receiving back the negative energy you emit towards others. It will always reflect back to you whether you are aware of it or not.

How do you change this habit—this restraining force within yourself—of being ungrateful? Start thinking about what you *are* grateful for—*right now*!

The Source of Gratitude

My intent is to live a life that reflects the values and ideals I want for my sons, friends, co-workers, and acquaintances. I desire my words to speak truth and foster only positive things such as encouragement, opportunities, and love. I'm not sure how many times you've experienced "foot-in-mouth" disease, but I've suffered through my share of the affliction. It always seems that we hurt those we care about the most. At times I find it harder to show my gratitude to those who need to see and hear it from me the most.

While reflecting on this, I discovered a related pattern within myself. I grew up hearing less praise and gratitude than I would have liked, which led to low self-esteem. As a result, I developed the habit of deflecting praise whenever it *was* given to me. I would often respond, "it was nothing" or "I didn't do as well as I would have liked." I never fully accepted praise from others—I would not let it in. Unconsciously, I didn't feel worthy of it, regardless of how hard I had worked or how well I had done. Ironically, affirmation is what I thrive on the most and what drives my behavior.

This habit of mine was brought to light one afternoon during a break between learning sessions in my Master's program. My friend, Noreen, paid me a compliment regarding something I had done and instead of accepting the compliment, letting it in and allowing myself to feel good about it, I diminished it with some self-deprecating comment. Her reaction was unlike anything I had experienced to that point in my life.

Her expression turned to a mixture of anger and sadness as she let me know—strongly—that my dismissiveness had insulted her. Here I was, receiving positive feedback from my learning partner and valued friend—someone who meant a great deal to me—*and I wasn't accepting it.*

The very thing I longed for—praise, recognition, and acceptance—I was not allowing myself to receive. Rather, I was attracting unwelcome feedback.

This was somewhat of an epiphany for me. I was thirty-seven years into my life and finally learned that *I* was preventing myself from feeling appreciated and loved. I was denying myself the affection and encouragement I craved and the ability to feel good about myself.

What was missing? Why was I reflecting this lack of gratitude onto others? Whoa—*why couldn't I accept myself?*

It is said that to love, you must first love yourself. To show gratitude, you must feel grateful. I wasn't loving myself. I wasn't feeling gratitude for my life's circumstances. I was appreciating all that I had—my wife, family, and work. I *was* appreciating what I was learning, however, it was tough to take it all in and begin to adapt to who I was when I left the relative safety of the learning environment.

So where does gratitude come from? How can you gain a sense of peace within yourself? When someone pays you a compliment, how can you learn to just say "thank you" without discounting the other person?

I believe that it comes from within yourself. When you can let go of the past and let go of your beliefs about yourself, you can allow new thoughts and feelings to enter your life and you can rewire your thinking. Moreover, you can attract new, positive experiences into your life by your very thoughts, feelings, and actions.

Gratitude begins with appreciating all that you have and all that you are. The gifts and talents you have been given in this life; the life experiences that have shaped who you are. Today I can live with contentment, knowing that I am the creator of my experience. I attract into my experience what I want, whether I am aware of it or not.

In order to be grateful to those around me and to let them know that I am grateful for them, I must first be grateful to myself. I must allow others to show their gratitude towards me so that I, in turn, express gratitude towards them.

The Power of Daily Habits

To achieve these goals, I have created some daily habits. For example, I begin each day by reading a devotional. This gets my mind and heart centered in a place to be my best as I greet the day.

Another habit I practice is focusing on what I am grateful for when I go to sleep and as I arise. When I first began this habit, I would write down at least three things I was grateful for. Lately it's grown to almost ten each morning. These are usually the names of people or recent experiences that made a positive impact on me. Sometimes I'll shoot them a quick text to let them know that I was thinking about them and that I am grateful for them.

Later in the morning I try to hand write at least two notes to business acquaintances or personal friends each day. It's usually a follow-up about a conversation we've had or a note of congratulations for something significant that happened in their lives.

Research shows that writing personal notes is even more powerful than we might realize—not only for the recipient, but also the sender. Taking the time to write personal notes creates positive thoughts and feelings of gratitude. We are blessed in the process of writing and sending love and encouragement to others, which is then reflected and multiplied with the recipients when they receive it.

As you can see, I was able to change my life. I have become more grateful and I am now frequently able to give and show my gratitude to others. You can, too. I encourage you to begin—right now!

MARIA'S VIEW

As I recovered from my knee injury, I had to relearn so many things. In physical therapy, I worked to get my range of motion back, to learn how to squat again, to climb up and walk down stairs. I remember exiting the gym with my walker and laughing because the little old ladies beat me going down the stairs to our cars.

Every movement required me to be intentional and calculated or it would bring forth shooting pain.

And through that, I learned gratitude. I learned the beauty of what I now call "gift moments." Our lives are made up of many ordinary moments: dinner with friends at a pub, watching a movie with a family member, workouts at the gym, watching a sunset or sunrise. We go about our busy lives and don't really think much about these events. I have learned though, that those underappreciated moments are typically the moments we later would love to get back.

When you're recovering from an injury, everything is a win. Your flexibility increased by one degree? Massive win! You're walking pain free? Yes, please! You're able to take a shower by yourself? Heck yes! These all became gift moments. I would literally stop and say "Hang on, can we take a moment to appreciate this for a second?"

It's funny when I think about it now, but that practice has become so ingrained in me that many times a day I'll stop what I'm doing, close my eyes, breathe a prayer of gratitude, and take a mental picture before I go on with life.

My roommates Christine and Kara were also my colleagues. Together we started a band and women's ministry that enabled us to travel all over the U.S., singing and speaking at women's events. Soon, we developed a routine: when we returned from the airport, we would buy sushi, Halo Top ice cream, and kombucha to take home. Then we would sit on the couch or floor, turn on a good chick flick, eat our food, and give each other massages. Many times we would say to each other, "You know, one day we're all going to be wives and moms. When we're up in the middle of the night nursing a baby, we'll think back to what a gift season this is!"

Lo and behold, a few years later, Kara married and had a baby. Soon afterward, she texted Christine and me in the middle of the night. "You guys remember how we talked about one day we would be up nursing a baby and remember those precious days when we all lived together and traveled and did all the things? Well tonight is that night...I'm so grateful to be a wife and mom now and wouldn't trade it for the world, but I'm also so grateful for that season we had together. It was special and such a gift."

Ahh . . . gift moments. They're all around us if we're willing to stop and look for them. What would happen if we started calling out those moments of gratitude in the moment? *How* do we do that?

I think we do it by recognizing that every moment contains a gift to be discovered. Granted, sometimes we don't see the gift in it until much later (like my knee injury experience!) but the more we proactively look for the gifts, the more we see them in our everyday moments.

What's amazing is the discovery that the more I'm grateful, the more things I find to be grateful about. I am literally programming my brain and my body to see the beauty, the good, and the things that are gifts (which is pretty much everything, if we have the eyes to see it!).

It was a process to walk this journey of appreciation, gratefulness, and gift moments, but now it's second nature. When you fully appreciate that there are only twenty-four hours deposited in our daily "time bank account," you suddenly realize how special your moments are.

I encourage you to find something today that you can "call out the good" on; something you can see as a gift moment. It can be as simple as a hot cup of coffee in the morning or a beautiful conversation with your spouse or a lovely rose in the garden. It doesn't have to be anything massive. What matters is your ability to recognize it as a gift. Think about it, feel it, breathe it in. This concerted effort changes your brain for the better.

Finding Focus

In June 2016, we were on the third day of backpacking along El Camino de Santiago and were still only in the French Alps. My traveling companion, Monica, and I weren't super close (she was better friends with one of my brothers at the time) but we were close enough and knew each other to be a "great person to travel with." This is really important because your travel buddy can enhance the experience or make it more challenging. I feel so blessed because Mon was the perfect travel sister.

Nevertheless, what had initially seemed like a brilliant idea was quickly morphing into the thoughts of *What made me think this was a good idea?* and *How did I get here?*

Technically, I could blame a boring psychology professor my freshman year of college. As his voice faded into the background, I began making what I fondly call "my list." At that moment, I began jotting down all the things I wanted to do in life, the places I wanted to go, and the experiences I wanted to have. I included everything I could think of; if it sounded like a good adventure or cool out-of-the-comfort-zone experience, onto the list it went!

The Camino was included because I had overheard some upperclassmen who had studied abroad talking about it. This 877-kilometer trek (almost 545 miles) across the French Alps and throughout Spain sounded exciting. According to tradition, it's the "Way of St. James"—the path he took to spread the gospel. Thus, every year, hundreds of thousands of people make the memorable (if not life-changing) pilgrimage from one end of the Camino to the other. I wanted to do so, too!

It took about fourteen years before I finally decided to conquer the Camino, which coincided with me just coming out of a rather sad and traumatic season of life. There's nothing like working through tough stuff by having hours upon hours to walk, think, and pray.

The first several days took us through the Pyrenees Mountains. Initially it was sheer excitement mixed with anticipation and a little bit of nervousness from not knowing exactly what to expect. But then as we kept going, I found myself focusing less on the beautiful scenery and more on the blisters on my feet and the unseasonably cold temperatures (for which we weren't prepared).

At one point, I realized I had better change what I was focusing on. This is where gratitude kicked into play. I could focus on the facts that my feet hurt, my shoulders ached from carrying my pack for hours and hours, and we still had hundreds of miles to go *or* I could focus on the facts that I was doing something that had been on my bucket list for a long time, I was out in glorious nature, I was meeting incredible people, and I was on the adventure of a lifetime.

Both thought trajectories were true, but one led to frustration and complaining while the other filled my heart with deep gratitude. I chose gratitude then, and I continue to do so today anytime I find myself in a negative spiral.

Gratitude is a choice; an intentional choosing of what to focus on. Consider how we can have the most amazing day with everything good happening *until* someone says one critical thing to us, or someone cuts us off in traffic, or any other little annoying thing happens. Then, suddenly, the entire day is ruined because that one negative thing consumes us.

I've been working with, coaching, and mentoring women in various capacities for about twenty years now and see this all the time. Many times when my clients share their thoughts about their struggles, I notice that they are focusing on—even clinging to—the one or two aspects that are making them miserable. When I ask why they are focusing on those specific things they tell me, "Well, because they're true!" I then pose the question, "Okay, so maybe those thoughts are true, but do you *want* to keep focusing on them? Out of the thousands of thoughts you could be thinking right now about this situation, wouldn't you rather choose thoughts that make you feel better about it?"

One thing that pains me greatly is when they focus on misperceptions about God. Many of them asked the Lord at one point in their lives to "use them" to do great things in the Kingdom (e.g., be a light, to serve, etc.). Initially they felt God used them in beautiful ways to make a difference, but now they feel as though they have been forgotten, even misused and discarded.

This highlights the importance of language, for us to be men and women of distinction in our words. And the distinction between the meanings of "use" is critical, especially after hearing clients share these thoughts over and over again, often said through tear-filled eyes. Perhaps we need to stop asking God to "use" us.

While I understand the sentiment behind it, and it even sounds really holy and beautiful, the reality is that things are to be used but people are to be loved! We were created from Love, for Love, and to Love. In contemplating this, I came to the realization that perhaps a better prayer is, "Lord, let me be your instrument."

What's the difference? As a musician, my instrument is my baby! I take good care of it, even when I'm not actively playing it. Instruments become beautiful when played by a good musician and kept in tune (there are so many analogies that could be made here!). I don't know any musicians who discard their instrument; they always care what happens to it because they love it. The same context can be applied to us because we are "instruments" for the Lord.

The Science of Gratitude

As I was thinking about being an instrument for the Lord, I read a book called *Sound Medicine* by Kulreet Chaudhary, MD on the science of sound and how it impacts the human body, based off of research in biophysics (sonocytology) by Dr. James Gimzewski, a Scottish physicist and professor of chemistry at the University of California. While I wouldn't necessarily recommend the whole book, the one part that stood out to me was that every bone, organ, and cell has its own resonant frequency and that together they make up a composite frequency for the body. It's as though each one were playing a different instrument that makes up a beautiful orchestra.

But how, you might be wondering, does science pertain to *gratitude*? Why does it really matter whether you're grateful or not? And does gratitude actually do anything good for you physically?

There is real scientific evidence that proves gratitude is extremely impactful to both our health and well-being. Gratitude can help reduce stress and depression, increase resilience, and strengthen relationships. It's been found that the more grateful people are, the greater their life satisfaction and overall well-being. They're also more likely to have better sleep, lower blood pressure, and stronger immune systems. Grateful people have a higher capacity for joy and positive emotions, tending to also make them more generous, happier, alert, and compassionate.

When the brain feels gratitude, the ventral and dorsal medial prefrontal cortex are all activated. Why is that important? Those are the areas that are involved in feelings of reward, positive social interactions, morality, interpersonal bonding, and the ability to understand what others are feeling or thinking.

Gratitude can also increase various important neurochemicals. When we shift from thinking negatively to positively, there is a surge of feel-good chemicals released such as dopamine, serotonin, and oxytocin. These contribute to the feelings of connection, happiness, and closeness that is often associated with gratitude.

This is probably why we are more grateful for things we do and the experiences we have than the things we possess. Our memories of positive experiences are always held strongly in our minds and our emotions.

The positive influence of gratitude on mental health continues past a particular event if the emotion is re-lived; subjects who participated in writing letters of gratitude for three months showed both behavioral increase in gratitude and significantly greater neural modulation by gratitude in the medial prefrontal cortex.

Amazingly, research has shown that this lasting effect is psychologically protective. In adolescents, feelings of gratitude have shown a decrease in bullying victimization and suicide risk. In other words, the regular practice of gratitude promotes compassion for others and an improved sense of our own self-worth.

Newton's Second Law as It Relates to Gratitude

Newton's second law explains how the velocity of an object changes when it is subjected to an external force. Because force is the product of an object's mass and its acceleration,[6] the change in velocity depends on the mass of the object. A force will cause a change in velocity; and likewise, a change in velocity will generate a force. The equation works both ways.

I think of gratitude as the velocity changer of our minds. Once we've made a decision to change and we move forward, gratitude becomes the accelerant that propels us with an even greater velocity. No matter what our circumstances are, there is always something to be grateful for. We need to seek out those things and remember that if we focus on what we are grateful for already, we'll start to see more things to be grateful for, and more good things will come into our lives. Eventually we won't be able to help but see more of the goodness all around us.

---

6. $F=m*a$

> **Gratitude becomes the accelerant that propels us with an even greater velocity.**

Gratitude has the added power of initiating a social loop that has the potential to expand the good for everyone involved. The more gratitude we feel, the more we'll act in a positive way toward others, which will prompt them to appreciate our behavior and engage more with us.

This beautiful cycle of gratitude strengthens our connections with others, reinforces generous behavior, and acknowledges appreciation—all of which serve to increase our confidence, push out negative thoughts, and become more positive.

The Power of Gratitude

Since gratitude builds on itself, consistency is key. It is important to practice gratitude daily. Our brains adapt and when they do, they go looking for the next good thing. Remember, what we focus on expands.

However, we want to practice gratitude for different things each day. Being grateful for the same things every day, even if they are important and worthy of deep appreciation, won't have the same effect on the brain as finding something positive and new each time.

Gratitude rewires our brain so that we become more likely to focus on the positives in the world than the negatives. While I'm not denying that negative and challenging things happen and one might argue that to only focus on the good things is unrealistic, I hear you; I am simply offering the concept that recognizing and appreciating the gifts in front of us helps us continue moving forward and enduring our challenging or painful emotions and circumstances.

The two can coexist; a person can have challenging, painful things going on in their life yet still look for and acknowledge the beauty and good that is present. The data supports this and shows that when we appreciate the positive in our lives, we become more open to the good things that nurture our happiness and well-being and, in the process, we see more beautiful things to be grateful for.

Looking in the Mirror

Each morning, we look in the mirror as we prepare to go out and face the world. What is our mindset as we look at our reflection? Are we grateful for the things that happened the previous day—even the challenges we may have had? Are we feeling like a victim or a creator?

Try to find gratitude even amid the challenging moments. Life is happening "for you" not "to you." Let's embrace the good challenges, start focusing on being grateful, and look forward to the blessings heading our way!

We now know that gratitude literally changes your brain and impacts how you experience the world and those around you. If you are intentional about practicing gratitude daily, you *will* live a happier, more fulfilled life! So what are you grateful for today?

JOURNAL EXERCISE

Are you a grateful person?

_____

Do you intentionally look for things to be grateful for, especially when you're having a challenging moment?

_____

If not, what would be different if you looked for something to be grateful for during a hard moment?

_____

_____

_____

Here's an interesting question: If tomorrow all you have is what you are grateful for today, what will you have tomorrow?

_____

_____

_____

Every day (morning and evening), write out at least five things you're grateful for!

1. _____

2. _____

3. _____

4. _____

5. _____

6. _____

7. _____

8. _____

9. _____

10. _____

CHAPTER 3

"May the God of hope fill you with all joy and peace as your trust in him, so that you may overflow with hope by the power of the Holy Spirit" —Romans 15:13

"The past is your lesson. The present is your gift. The future is your motivation." —Unknown

---

Feel the happiness now you imagine it will be when....

TIM'S VIEW

I had taken up Latin dancing as a new hobby, taking lessons once or twice a week for several months. Salsa, Bachata, a little Cha-Cha, Merengue, and Kizomba, too. I'd come to love it so much that I began dancing socially two to three times a month. After I progressed to intermediate-level classes, I was determined to become a "Salsero," an expert leader at Salsa dancing. I even purchased a pair of dancing shoes that offered the smoothest motion on the dance floor.

Dancing with specific partners spurred me to increase my skill level and focus. I visualized certain turn combinations and other skills that I could lead with confidence. In my mind, I saw myself and my dance partner thoroughly enjoying ourselves in the dance. I was enjoying meeting new people within our dance community and making new friendships as a result of this and I eagerly anticipated my inaugural participation in the annual Port City Salsa Splash.

But then COVID-19 hit.

Not only was the dance canceled, but all other events and nonessential businesses also closed—including the dance studio. I had no idea how much I truly enjoyed dancing and its healthy benefits until it all went away for about six months.

The studio owner pivoted her business to online classes, which were interesting, but they didn't feed my soul like actually dancing with a partner. Then she started to host some outdoor footwork classes, with social distancing in place. A few weeks later, she added some Salsa and Bachata partner-work classes where we only danced with one specific partner, as opposed to rotating partners in a normal class format. I didn't care; I was ready to get back to moving towards my goal of being a Salsero!

I invited a friend, whom I'll call "Mary," from the studio to partner with me at one of these classes. I selected her not only for her fun personality and ready smile but also because she was competitive and focused on getting the steps and counting down first and foremost. She encouraged me to take my skills up a notch to become a better leader for her. That one-night class brought me tremendous joy.

Not long after that, the studio reopened for dedicated partner work. It was a beginner's class but I really wanted the opportunity to dance with Mary again. Although we were not beginners per se, we were relatively new to dancing together so the instructor approved our partnership.

We had tremendous fun together but at the conclusion of the first class, the lead male instructor spoke with us specifically about our connection. Physical connection is so important in Salsa dancing—any kind of dancing, for that matter. I'm amazed at the level of connection that occurs with a dance partner physically, mentally, and emotionally. If I'm leading, I have to be fully present to signal to my dance partner where I would like her to move in order to accomplish a step and execute my intentions. But it is really just an invitation—a suggestion. She will usually accept the invitation and execute the maneuver if I provide a clear signal. But if my intentions are not adequately conveyed, or she is not fully present and paying attention to my signal, something completely different may occur.

He shared how I could be more effective as a leader and how she could be more effective as a follower. If I wanted to become a confident leader, I needed to connect with her better.

When she and I spoke later that week, I shared that I believed I could CONNECT with her better by:

- Communication better with her non-verbally,
- Orienting my focus on her,
- Noticing our spacing,
- Not judging either of us,
- Establishing better eye contact with her,
- Creating safe space, and her
- Trusting my abilities to lead.

These insights apply to other life situations beyond dancing, such as goal setting. We don't live in isolation and we shouldn't try to attain our goals on our own, either. When we CONNECT with others in an honoring way, we'll get farther, faster:

- Communicate at all times.
- Orient ourselves with our surroundings.
- Notice those who walk with us.
- Never judge ourselves or others when mistakes are made.
- Eye our emotions; nip negative ones in the bud.
- Create safe space to both work and unwind.
- Trust in ourselves—and our leaders—to attain our goals.

WHAT BRINGS YOU JOY?

I love music. I love listening to it, singing with it, and leading others in song. I enjoy writing songs and playing my guitar in a band; I get a rush from the applause of the audience when they enjoy my performance. This brings me happiness.

When I'm in a good mood, I often catch myself humming or singing a song. My favorite part of a church service is always the praise and worship time. I feel alive with music.

However, some music is not as uplifting as others. I'll now switch radio stations to find something more positive and uplifting if I sense a song's lyrics or mood are altering my happy outlook.

What causes you to feel happy? What activities bring you joy? Can you identify them?

Maybe it's your spouse or lover holding you in their arms. Maybe it's the joy of seeing your son or daughter or grandchild at work or play. Or maybe it's as simple as your dog or cat jumping onto your lap. Whatever it is, this is what you want to deliberately focus on.

Your power to create the life you want is in the present moment—right now. Increasing your happiness—your financial and physical well-being—will be manifested as a result of the thoughts and feelings you are having right now.

If you look in the mirror and like what you see, you are happy.

Have you ever imagined something significant that you wanted in your life? Were you uplifted by this or were you feeling deflated conjuring up reasons for "why not" in your mind? Bring your dreams into the now by taking action, eliminating any fear, and engaging your natural genius. By taking action, your self-esteem is uplifted and you acquire increased abilities as you take each new action. When you focus on feeling the happiness *now*, you empower your emotions and intentions to bring about the change you want to create for yourself.

Living in the Present

Ever notice how easily we can be distracted? When talking with someone, our mind races ahead to how we are going to answer their question or share our opinion. Or, worse yet, we completely tune them out and think about something else entirely.

One night I was Salsa dancing with one of my instructors at a social event. I noticed the smile on her face so I allowed myself to enjoy the moment as the song progressed.

When the song concluded, we embraced. I stepped back and said, "I realized something as we danced. You get a kick out of seeing me improve." She let out a loud, "Yes!"

At that moment I had total clarity. What brought her as much joy as the dance itself was to see me, her student, improve and experience the same joy. In addition to the growing joy I felt towards dancing, I also grew in confidence from her teaching and the level of understanding between us. I treasure that "gift moment." It took our relationship as teacher and student to a deeper level of commitment and joy. All this came about by merely being present; by noticing the subtlety of a slightly different smile in the presence of the one I was with.

When we are with another person we can sense their level of presence with us by their body language as much as anything. How much have we missed out on being present with the person we are with?

The Power of Emotions

Are you a person who is normally happy and excited about what the day will bring? Or do you dread getting up in the morning and all you'll have to face? Did you know that the very emotion you are feeling right now is determining your future? I'm not saying we aren't going to have moments of anger, disappointment, or sadness. But I'm talking about your underlying sense of contentment, your outlook, what you are working towards, and your dreams.

Are you tuned in to the emotional cues of your body? I have found that, generally, when I feel things welling up in my chest, they are emotions that reflect love, happiness, and joy. When I feel things sinking down in my chest, they are directed towards fear, sadness, or things like regret.

An emotion can be defined scientifically as a conscious mental reaction subjectively experienced as a strong feeling; an affective aspect of our consciousness. In laymen's terms, it's our body's physical response to the thoughts we are thinking in our minds. Or, more simply put: what we think is what we feel. Consider our emotional responses to dreams, movies, advertisements, books, and stories. As Maria previously explained, the circumstances to which we are responding aren't real yet our minds process and react to them as if they are.

Compare it to throwing a pebble into water. The pebble is the thought (or the cause) and the ripples are your emotions (the effect).

Some common misconceptions regarding emotions include:

- They just come out of nowhere and happen to us.

- There is no point to emotions.

- There are good and bad emotions.

- Emotions are not a choice and many people incorrectly say that they have no control over them.

- If I want to be holy or strong, I need to ignore my emotions.

I actually become stronger by acknowledging my feelings and the thoughts associated with them. When I recognize that I can consciously and intentionally change my thoughts about any situation, I recognize that my thoughts are optional, and thus I can have a different emotional response then I might have had to the same situation now from similar circumstances in the past.

How to "Embrace the Suck"

When I was a U.S. Army officer, I had the privilege—and challenge—of completing the Army's Ranger program. Ranger school is one of the toughest training courses for which a soldier can volunteer. For sixty-one days, trainees are pushed to their mental and physical limits in a variety of locations and terrains.

Conceived during the Korean War, the purpose of the Ranger course is to prepare these Army volunteers—both officers and enlisted soldiers—to become skilled leaders within close combat and direct-fire battles.

It was during this training that I first encountered the phrase, "embrace the suck." In military jargon, this means to consciously accept or appreciate something that is extremely unpleasant but unavoidable. Sometimes in life we encounter circumstances that we'd prefer not to be in, but we need to press forward and get through it.

Consider our various seasons of suffering: A period of singleness until we find our spouse. A period of grieving following the loss of a family member or friend. A period of heartbreak. A period of illness.

I can recall the fear and sense of helplessness my former wife and I felt when she was diagnosed with breast cancer. Yet she educated herself and remained optimistic about the outcome while we found the best care possible. I admired her courage in how she dealt with the process. She came through it with flying colors and remains cancer free.

About a year later I was helping a client sell her home. She was also battling breast cancer and was working with the same oncologist and plastic surgeon team my wife had used. I shared my wife's experience and the concept of "embrace the suck;" I even bought her a t-shirt emblazoned with the phrase. The client, too, successfully beat her cancer; she embraced her suck boldly.

Being BOLD in the Face of Fear

While writing this book, I told Maria that I was struggling with what to share about one of my particular experiences in one of the chapters. She suggested that I listen to Brené Brown, a popular author, speaker, and researcher who talks about vulnerability and shame, and recommended that I specifically listen to her TED Talk, "Power of Vulnerability."

I had listened to it once before but decided to follow Maria's suggestion and listened again. I also reviewed Brené's speech, "Listening to Shame." The second talk especially hit home; it allowed me to realize what was holding me back in my writing: past shame.

I then realized that I feared losing my connection with Maria. If she knew some of the parts of my past, would she still want to collaborate with me on this project? Our literary partnership had become incredibly important to me because of the things she was teaching me and her encouragement. More than this, I valued her friendship.

This is when I discovered that believing in yourself is very important to be able to imagine your future state. Sometimes we just need to act as if we already have the self-confidence we need to accomplish what we've imagined. And sometimes we have to borrow the belief that is lacking within ourselves from a friend or family member who has confidence in our abilities.

So Maria and I had a conversation. I introduced the BOLD acrostic I had created as a way to help me to share my thoughts and relay my fears:

- B = I am Brave.

- O = I take the Opportunity.

- L = I come from a place of Love.

- D = I am Determined/Diligent.

I was honored by her grace. I was so grateful for her incredible ability to remain present and hold space for what was a very vulnerable conversation for me. It not only strengthened both our collaboration and our ability to relate to one another as friends, but it was also crucial to my ability to dig into the stories of my life that would benefit you, the reader.

I'm reminded of the introduction to the *Star Trek* television show of my youth: "Space, the final frontier / These are the voyages of the starship *Enterprise* / Its five-year mission / To explore strange new worlds / To seek out new life / And new civilizations / To boldly go where no man has gone before."[7]

As we grow, sometimes we must embrace new challenges. We must get uncomfortable at times. If we are willing to face things that have scared us in the past, we can have incredible growth. A feeling of self-confidence can emerge. Feelings of joy and happiness with newfound perspectives are given rise from a new mindset. When I think about how happy and grateful I am for changes

---

7.   https://genius.com/Star-trek-star-trek-opening-lyrics. Narration by William Shatner. Realease date: September 8, 1966. Written by Gene Roddenberry and Alexander Courage. All three seasons aired on the NBC network.

I have made, or are making, I can look forward with expectancy and feel now what I imagine it will be when….

MARIA'S VIEW

When I began strategic mindset and life coaching, one of the things that seemed to be most challenging for my clients was going from a new thought to a new feeling. If we want to create something different in our lives, we have to have a new thought, which leads to a new feeling, which leads to new behavior, which ultimately leads to a new experience. But sometimes it's challenging to connect the new thought with a feeling; to really feel it.

During that time I learned of a concept that I like to call 'stair-step thoughts." In order to get your brain to accept a new thought as even a possibility, you select a stair step thought to bridge between what you think now and the thought you ultimately want to believe.

For example, maybe your thought is '*I hate my body!*' but you want to get to '*I love my body!*' When you think '*I hate my body!*' that thought feels 100 percent true and when you think '*I love my body!*' it feels 100 percent false. That is when you need a stair step thought! A thought that your brain says *Hmm… this* could *be true; I can get on board with the possibility of this thought.*

So a stair step thought in this example could be '*I have a body!*' Then every time your brain starts to go to '*I hate my body!*' you immediately take that thought captive and replace it with '*I have a body!*' and you work on practicing that thought until it feels 100 percent true.

There are different conclusions as to how long it takes to create new neural pathways of thought. Some say it takes 66 days, some say it takes less than that, while still others say it takes 100 days. Regardless, what we do know is that it takes consistent thinking of this new thought in order to hardwire it. So if you stick with it, eventually you will get to a place where you can say, "I *love* my body!" and feel it to be true. So keep practicing the new thought until you feel it and believe it!

Be Vulnerable

While growing up, I was never told "don't cry!" nor did I hear the message, "Be tough; don't cry." Yet, surrounded by brothers full of testosterone who exhibited a certain "toughness" day in and day out, I simply took it as the norm. Things such as jumping off fifty-foot cliff ledges into the water below, figuring out how to make explosives with various household items, and accidentally setting fire to trees created a certain mental toughness. Because of that, I grew up thinking, *What's the point of crying, unless you absolutely can't hold it in?*

While this mindset may have served me well in my childhood growing up in a household of boys, I later realized if we push away the pain of life, we also push away the joy. This came to my attention in college as I was watching a movie with some friends. When a really sad part came on, my friends allowed tears to stream down their faces while I held mine in. As I looked at them, I suddenly realized these friends were living authentically in a way that I hadn't allowed myself to experience ... until that moment. As I allowed the tears to fall, I experienced a sensation of freedom and transparency; a moment of truly letting myself be "human" in all that it entailed. It was beautiful and real and raw.

If we push away the pain of life, we also push away the joy.

Since then, I have come to realize that the strongest people I know are those who allow the tears to flow when the situation (or movie or book!) elicits such a response. It actually takes far more courage to let yourself feel and express a deep feeling (in an appropriate way), than it does to push it away and act "tough."

I've learned so much about the courage of tears through my fiance, Matt, who (by the time you are reading this, will be my husband!) both laughs and cries easily and is the most authentic person I've ever met and is one of the strongest men I know.

The people I admire most now are the ones who express authenticity. We are meant to be whole, fully integrated human beings and when we choose thoughts and emotions that match, it can be a powerful tool for making unifying changes internally and in the world.

Feel. Be. Experience.

The Power of Mental Rehearsal

Between the ages of eight and eighteen, I took piano lessons. My teacher thought I was capable of excelling at the piano so she insisted I compete in classical recitals. While I should have been honored and excited, I dreaded it. I didn't like playing classical music and despite my super competitive personality, I didn't want to compete in music (athletics was a different story).

Since I couldn't avoid the performances, I decided I might as well get blue ribbons. So I practiced at the piano during the day and in my head while in bed at night. I imagined myself performing at the recital, playing it perfectly and getting a blue ribbon before "peacing out" of there! (I know it wasn't the best attitude, but you get the point.)

The crazy thing is, as much as I hated playing at these recitals, I always did really well. I don't believe it was because I was an exceptional classical pianist; trust me, I wasn't! No, I believe it was because I mentally rehearsed as if it were already happening.

We know through neuroscience that when you imagine something and work on feeling it, the brain and body can't tell the difference whether it is actually happening or imagined. It's the same reason why when we watch a scary movie, our heart rate speeds up. Even though we know we are safe, it registers in our brain that what is happening in the movie is actually happening to us at that moment.

I'm always telling my clients that our thoughts are our God-given "superpowers;" ones that He has given us to make sure we have the ability to choose to be a victor rather than a victim in our lives! I believe we have barely tapped into the power of what He has given us.

Our thoughts have the potential to help us live lives of freedom.

Walking Into Your Dream

One of my favorite things about the work I do is seeing people's lives completely transformed. One such client's story ties in so deeply with the "feel now what you imagine when…." that I have to share it here (with her permission). It highlights the incredible power of our beliefs, which are the thoughts we keep repeating to ourselves until they become truth to our brains.

In one of the first meetings with "Mary," we discussed what she would like to think and believe about herself, and how she would like to show up in a room. She'd had trauma and abuse in her background, which had resulted in physical limitations. "What I'd really love to do is be able to walk without my walker or my cane," she said. "But I'm disabled, so … oh, well."

"Wait a second, " I replied. "You just said you wanted to be able to walk without assistance, but in that same breath you claimed disability over your life. From a brain/body perspective, that's super confusing. Why don't you just start saying, believing, and visualizing that you are fully healed and that you can walk and run without a cane or a walker? Can you see yourself doing those things?"

She could.

So we began to work on her internal scripts (the things she would say about herself), various mind-management tools, and some simple movement exercises I had developed over the years as a personal trainer. Every day she wrote down her dream of being able to walk into a room without limping or needing help.

About a month into this work, we held a Zoom meeting together. As soon as she saw my face appear on the screen, she excitedly announced, "Maria! Watch this!"

She turned the computer camera towards the hallway, got up, and walked up and down the hallway without her cane or walker! My eyes filled with tears. She was experiencing what she had envisioned herself doing! What she had been mentally rehearsing was actually happening.

To say that her life was radically changed is an understatement. She has since gone skydiving, walking miles and miles around her neighborhood, bike riding, and is currently training for a Spartan Race!

There have been so many beautiful stories of people who mentally rehearsed various things such as golf or music and when they actually did those things, they nailed them! Why? Because the brain can't distinguish between what has happened in the past, what is happening now, or what is going to happen in the future. It only registers thoughts as happening now, in that moment.

This is why it is so important to be very cognizant of what thoughts we allow to take up residence in our minds. I always tell my clients "If you don't want that thought to actually happen, then don't think it!"

Why? Because when you think a thought, it impacts your feelings, then your actions and then turns into results in your life. You will subconsciously go towards what you are thinking about. It's the way God made our bodies and brains work. When we think intentional thoughts, that's so powerful because we are using the gift God gave us well. But when we let our thoughts run us, we are not being good stewards of this gift. A mind unchecked with thoughts that are running rampant is like letting a two-year old run around the house with a sharp knife; it's dangerous!

The brain can't distinguish between what is real and what is imagined

Our thoughts are literally our God-given super powers.

Here's what I mean by that statement: God made our bodies to work a certain way, Scripture says we are fearfully and wonderfully made.[8] The more I learn about our bodies and brains, the more I come to understand how true that verse is and how we've barely scratched the surface in utilizing the tools God gave us to live beautiful, healthy, and fulfilling lives for Him and others.

All throughout Scripture we are told about the power of our thoughts and words. There are numerous verses telling us to capture our thoughts, to be aware of what we are focusing on, and to be renewed in our minds. Why is that?

---

8.   Psalm 139:14

Because when we aren't aware of the power of our thoughts and aren't intentional about the thoughts we let in, they impact our lives in really negative ways. But when we do take responsibility for the gift of our thoughts and our minds and our words, it can be the most life-giving and life-changing experience!

I've seen many people read those verses and gloss over them saying, "Oh, that's nice," but not recognizing the gravity of what those scriptures mean. I was that person for years, reading those verses and having no idea how God was literally giving us access to a "superpower" that could help to transform our lives–physically and emotionally, not *just* spiritually.

We now know our thoughts impact our emotions, our hormones, our health, our actions, our relationships, and literally every single part of our lives. It's also the place where if we don't take responsibility for it rather than being a God-given superpower, it can become a death trap.

The Science of Thoughts

There have been many studies and books written on the impact of our thoughts in regard to our health. Our bodies are made to heal themselves when they are given what they need. God made us like a well-maintained car; take care of the car and it will usually run pretty well! But if we don't, we can crash and burn as a result.

Moral of the story: Understand the power that God has entrusted to you with your thoughts and be a good steward of that gift.

In addition to visualization, I recommend the following "I am" statement exercises to help you reach your goal:

1. In your mind, fast forward to the end of this year, pretending it's December 31st. What do you want to have accomplished by then? What goals or dreams do you want to have come to fruition? How do you want to have grown? Write those things down!

2. Begin to imagine those dreams and goals and things you want to accomplish as coming true. Who do you need to become and what do you need to believe about yourself in order to achieve those dreams? Write those things down!

3. Turn those into "I am" statements. For example, maybe you look at your dreams and realize you need to believe that you're brave, that you have what it takes, that you're worthy, and so forth. So you would write, "I am brave! I have what it takes! I am worthy!"

4. From here on out—three times a day—read aloud what you wrote, running your finger under the words so your eyes follow along (it helps to wire it deeply into your brain). It's also really powerful if you record yourself reading it and then listen to it as well.

Why is it so important to "emotionalize" our thoughts for change to take place? Because they cause neurochemical changes, some of which are temporary and some are long lasting. Studies have shown that when people intentionally practice gratitude, they get a surge of rewarding neurotransmitters such as dopamine. They then experience a general brightening and alerting of the mind that probably correlates with more of the neurochemical norepinephrine.

Our thoughts become "things" that take on flesh in a very real way.

Building Confidence

I've heard it said many times that "confidence comes with competence." I disagree. Sure, if I know how to do something well, I can feel more confident, but that confidence is dependent on external circumstances.

What's wrong with that? The problem is that I become a victim to my circumstances.

I propose a different perspective: Confidence comes from knowing who you are and your worth, *regardless* of your circumstances. And on that same note, you will rise and fall based off of what you believe about yourself.

> **Confidence comes from knowing who you are and your worth, *regardless* of your circumstances.**

Recently I was reminded of how true it is that confidence is an inside job. After moving to a new town, I randomly decided to go to a hip-hop class. Even though I had been a dancer growing up (a ballerina, which is *very different* from hip hop), I felt out of my element in this class in which everyone else knew each other *and* all the moves.

Over the next hour as I struggled to keep up, I realized I had a choice to make: I could withdraw into self-consciousness or I could step out into confidence by acknowledging that I was in a place of learning. I chose the latter.

During the last fifteen minutes of class, the teacher invited each student to do the choreographed dance as a solo. We didn't have to, but it was encouraged. As I watched the other students absolutely kill their dance routines, I pushed past my insecurities and said to myself, *You know what? I'm learning and that's amazing. I'm going to step into courage and that's brave!*

So I danced the solo! It wasn't great, but I held onto the confidence of knowing I'm worthy, not that I'm an incredible hip-hop dancer. My value and confidence isn't in getting something right; it's in choosing to step out into bravery regardless of the outcome.

Powerful Visualization Techniques

Visualization is the act of creating something first in our imagination; in a sense, it's inventing something in our minds. Scripture says without a vision the people perish. (Proverbs 29:18a) Therefore, visualizing is really the act of clarifying your desired destination. When we don't have a vision for our lives, we end up living a life of default rather than design. We all have an invitation from God to imagine a beautiful life, make a plan, and work the plan to make it a reality. Then we can turn around and give back to those around us. It's a beautiful cycle!

Visualization is powerful. There are several ways we can bring the power of imagination coupled with our emotions into visualization.

Some people use the process of "mirror work"—standing in front of a mirror and reading out their goals, again bringing the power of their emotions to visualizing it in the here and now. Another way is to write out our dreams and goals. Some people carry around a goal card in their pocket or purse, set a reminder on their calendar, and pull it out and read it at set times during the day.

You can do your goal card work while in your daily commute, walking your dog, or just going for a walk. If you're a jogger, you can record a series of life scripts, dreams/goals, and/or self-image scripts and combine them with the positive impact of improved health and fitness.

Voice recorders are another great tool where you can record and repeat your dreams, goals, or life script. Most smartphones have a voice memo app preinstalled on them. Some people will even record their voice track over an inspirational piece of music to bring even greater power to the process.

Another technique is to have a "nightstand question" such as "Now that my goal is fulfilled, how do I feel?" and let yourself imagine the answer to that question as you're falling asleep.

The key is repetition. This isn't a one-time thing; it's every day until the wish is fulfilled, then on to the next big dream. We know that top-level amateur and professional athletes have been using the power of visualization for years. There are so many studies to back this up; MIT neuroscientists have done some fascinating studies on the power of visualization and articles have been written in *Forbes*, *Huff Post*, and *Psychology Today* (to name a few) on the benefit of this practice. So, why not bring it into our everyday lives?!

Dreams Develop Your Affirmations

Our minds contain the power to overcome self-limiting beliefs but we need to give ourselves *permission* to dream! Our dreams are important because they fuel our discipline and give us our ability to persist. Without our dreams, we rob ourselves of maximizing our potential.

We need to focus on what makes our heart sing. What would you do if you knew you couldn't fail? What are the desires of your heart? Clarify them and then set the direction you want to go. Then you will achieve results. Clarity gives us freedom!

Clear dreams give us focus, get us excited, build our confidence, fulfill us, and grow us. When those dreams involve others, we are able to collaborate and create with mentors who keep us both motivated and humble—humility is the highest virtue.

Once we give ourselves permission to dream, we can reinforce our ability to achieve our dreams by building up our perception of ourselves. We need to have self-confidence because there are roadblocks to overcome, such as other people's opinions, undeveloped skills, fear, and stress. The good news is that fear is simply an opportunity to learn something new; maybe a new skill for example!

Below are a series of affirmations that may help you boost your confidence. Remember that your dreams begin in your imagination. If you want to feel it, you must think it first! Say to yourself:

- "I am a man/woman of vision and imagination!"
- "Feel now what you imagine it will be when."
- "I dream my painting, and then I paint my dream." (Vincent Van Gogh)
- "Imagination is more powerful than education." (Albert Einstein)

Our thoughts are the originator of everything we create. History is being written right now by people with imagination! Don't stop running towards your dream. When you go for what you love, you gain confidence as you take action.

- "I will run towards my dreams."
- "I believe in myself."
- "I'm going for what is mine!"
- "I'm worth it."
- "I'm going for what I love."
- "Who I am is God's gift to me; who I become is my gift back to God."
- "The most difficult thing I do, I do right away, because that's what winners do." (Ryan Donovan)

There are also consequences if we don't take action. For example, some of the biggest regrets people have while on their deathbeds are that they hadn't taken action and dove in headfirst, that they waited to "start it tomorrow" (because tomorrow never comes!), and that they hadn't taken more chances. Regret is a bitter pill to swallow.

But more than that, *you* are a gift in who you are and what you bring to the world. God created you that way and when you don't live your purpose, the world is robbed of that beauty and you are deprived of the joy of becoming even more of the incredible person you were created to be!

The Emotional Impact of Visualization

Have you ever had to give a presentation? As you mentally prepared for the event, perhaps your heart began beating faster or you felt yourself freaking out. The presentation hadn't happened yet but your body was responding in a way that would say it *was* actually happening. Why is that? Because when you imagine something and emotionalize it, your brain takes it as that *is* what is happening *now* and responds in kind.

When an emotion is linked to a thought, it becomes powerful.

Why is this important? Most of the time we are living out of our familiar and habitual thoughts, feelings, and actions and then we continually have the same attitude and life experience, which then loops back to restart the thought cycle.

For example, let's say in the morning I oversleep and I rush to get my clothes from the laundry room so I'm not late for work. But my husband forgot to put the clothes into the dryer, as he said he would. So when I open the dryer, it's empty—the clothes are still in the washing machine. I immediately think *Why didn't he do what he said he was going to do?! He never does what I ask him to do!*

That thought then creates a feeling of anger and frustration. My reticular activating system kicks into gear, helping me see more of what I'm focusing on. Suddenly, I'm thinking of all the things I'm frustrated with my husband about as I rush to get ready. I dash out of the house feeling super grouchy and ticked off at the world. When I get to work, I treat others poorly because I'm upset with my husband.

These people then get upset with me and act in kind, causing me to think how rude people are. When I get home at the end of the day, I lash out at my husband for him upsetting my whole day. He in turn gets angry and responds with impatience. I'm now convinced I have the worst life.

So I keep thinking more negative thoughts, which lead to more negative emotions. I start acting out in negative behaviors and keep achieving negative results. Before I know it, I'm not paying attention to what I'm doing or saying or thinking, because, well, clearly my life is just terrible and the world is full of terrible people. I'm simply running off of my habitual negative thoughts, emotions, actions, and results. When I feel it, I act it out.

To break that cycle, I have to think and do things differently.

When trying to "feel" a new vision for our lives, we tend to reference the past as our guide post. But if we are always looking backward, we will always end up reliving the past. We can be defined by a memory of the past or by a vision of the future; it's up to us to choose.

If you have a vision for the future but you're having a hard time "feeling it," try sitting in a comfortable position, close your eyes, and imagine the scene. What do you see? What do you hear? What are the smells around you in that vision? How would you feel if you were really there? Just practice it for a bit.

JOURNAL EXERCISE

What is your vision for your life? Where would you love it to be? What would you like to be doing? Who will you be doing it with? How will you feel when you're living your dream? What kind of emotions will you be feeling and what kind of thoughts will you be thinking?

_____

_____

_____

_____

_____

_____

Since we know that emotions fuel our actions, and our emotions come from our thoughts, we can then create the emotions we need to fuel our desired actions. Some emotions that we can use to get us into action are: curiosity, excitement, and creativity. Ask yourself, "What would I need to be thinking about to generate these emotions?"

_____

_____

_____

_____

_____

_____

CHAPTER 4

*"And over all these virtues put on love, which binds them
all together in perfect unity" —Colossians 3:14*

*"I find love much like a mirror. When I love another, he(she) becomes
my mirror and I become his(hers), and reflecting in each other's love
we see infinity!" —Leo Buscaglia, Love: What Life Is All About*

Love yourself and
let others know you love them

TIM'S VIEW

Learning how to love freely and appropriately can be a struggle, especially when
it has been withheld from us or used against us in the past. But if we open our
hearts and minds to the possibility of healthy love, we can experience it in its
truest form.

I didn't grow up in a family that expressed a lot of love or showed a
lot of outward affection. I recall interviewing my mother when I was about
thirty-five—she in her fifties—for a family of origin study I was working on
as part of my Master's program. I anticipated learning more about my mom,
especially what it was like for her growing up and her perspective of raising
my four brothers and me. I had not expected to learn that she and my dad had

consciously chosen to withhold physical affection from us boys when we were young because they didn't want to raise "sissies."

I was taken aback. The very thing that would have been the most nurturing and encouraging thing to me as a young boy was intentionally withheld for my supposed good. It was a startling revelation.

Raised in an Irish-Catholic family, I attended Mass every Sunday. My education included catechisms as a child, a private Catholic high school, and then a Jesuit university. My brothers and I were taught to always give a sturdy hand shake and to be respectful of parents, elders, teachers, and those in positions of authority. And while the *principles* of love were certainly taught throughout my upbringing, it just wasn't customary for my parents to display affection or offer words of praise or affirmation. (Unless you brought home a good report card. Dad was a school teacher and education was highly valued.)

It wasn't until I was a senior in high school that I began to initiate hugs with my parents and others. It was a practice I learned while serving as a co-leader at a religious retreat that year. Although my parents were uncomfortable with it at first, they eventually welcomed the hugs, which are now freely given at family gatherings.

The lack of affection at home didn't deter my healthy interest in girls as a teenager; I had girlfriends from about the time I was fifteen. However, I was awkward around members of the opposite sex and really didn't know how to relate to them. Thus, I developed a pattern in high school of breaking off relationships when my feelings got too strong. I just didn't know how to handle them.

To mask my insecurities and boost my self-confidence, I began to experiment with various substances, including alcohol. I began drinking regularly when I was in junior high (middle school), sneaking liquor from the kitchen cabinet. By the time I reached high school, I was attending keg parties after sporting events, often drinking more than I should. Let's just say I was not a model citizen in my youth.

My misplaced perceptions of love was the deciding factor for the university I attended. I was crazy about one of my high school classmates, who had also served on the religious retreat team our senior year. She was way out of my league as far as popularity goes and we only went on one date that spring before graduation, but to my mind, we seemed to have bonded.

Since she had been accepted to a private university about five hours east of our hometowns in the Seattle area, I applied and was accepted as well. We went on one date the first semester; it was clear that she did not have the same feelings towards me that I had for her. It threw me off course ... until I was introduced to someone else that fall.

"Jenny" (not her real name) and I dated throughout the rest of our freshman year; she even came to visit me in my hometown with one of her girlfriends that following summer. Then one day during the fall of our sophomore year, she asked to talk with me. Her eyes said it even before the words left her mouth. "I'm pregnant." As she cried, I held her and tried to comfort her. I felt so many emotions all at once: scared, ashamed, guilty. What were we going to do?

Since neither of us were willing to face being parents, we decided to end the pregnancy with an abortion. It was a horrible event for both of us; to this day, this is what I am most ashamed of.

Afterward, every time I looked at her, I was reminded of what felt like the biggest mistake I'd ever made in my life. Every month when I paid the medical bill I received in my student mailbox, the shame was reinforced. Our relationship soon ended.

I didn't possess good self-esteem prior to this happening and the guilt and shame of the abortion took me to an even lower place.

Sometimes our lowest points are the springboard to our greatest growth.

Yet sometimes our lowest points are the springboard to our greatest growth. When we feel powerless over a situation, it is a perfect opportunity to make a shift in mindset. For me, I draw upon my faith. When I feel powerless,

I know that there is a power greater than my own that will help me reach a better place.

One tool I use is to identify the negative thought that I am having, reject it, and replace it with a healthier thought. Think of "The 3 R's":

1. Recognize that you are having a thought that does not serve you.

2. Reject it immediately.

3. Replace the thought with a positive and healthy one and get into action to make the change come about.

What is Love Frame of Reference

I can truly say that I've only experienced unconditional love twice in my life.

The first was when I was in my thirties, when I truly recognized the love of my Heavenly Father and his son, Jesus, who died on the cross for me and my sins. This is a love that is available to us all, should we choose to accept it. I did … and continue to hold onto it every day, even when I feel unworthy to receive it.

The second was with a woman I dated my senior year of college.

"Susan" (not her real name) and I first met as freshmen when we lived in the same co-ed dormitory. We didn't date then, but I remember she always wore a huge smile, had a quick wit, and was always engaging.

Jump forward to the spring of my sophomore year. It was Easter week and I attended a late-night mass service; Susan was also there with some of her friends. We spoke afterward and then reconnected at a party a week or two later. We dated a couple of times but since she was going to be studying in Florence, Italy our junior year, we just remained friends.

The spring semester of our senior year, Susan and I began dating again. By the end of the year, we were getting pretty serious as a couple. Because I had participated in the ROTC throughout college, I became a commissioned second lieutenant in the Army the day before I graduated with my Bachelor's degree; Susan still had one more semester to complete before she graduated.

I was immediately stationed at Fort Lewis, Washington, where I served as a training officer for the ROTC Advanced Camp before heading to the Field Artillery Officer Basic Course in Fort Sill, Oklahoma. Knowing that the Army would be my career for the next twenty years or so, I proposed to Susan and she accepted.

After I graduated from artillery school, I began the cross-country drive back to Washington. Along the way, I experienced the worst snowstorm the southwest had seen in ~100 years. I spent the next two days driving on compact snow or ice. Fortunately, Susan had mailed me a cassette of "windshield wiper" music ahead of my journey. I listened to it over and over as I drove and thought of seeing her.

After reuniting with her at the college, we followed each other in separate cars back to my hometown south of Seattle where we'd be spending the Christmas holidays with my family. I was going to attend Ranger school for a couple of months and then be sent to Korea for a year, so I needed to leave my car with my parents.

Susan taught me the expression "driving by Braille" as we drove west on I-90. This refers to the rumble strips cut as grooves along the freeway, the sound of which catch your attention when you drift out of your lane.

We enjoyed our time with my family over Christmas and then we began the drive south to her hometown in Saratoga, California where her parents threw us an engagement party. We were in an ethereal state of love and happily began to plan our future together. We decided to wait to get married until after I returned from Korea.

I graduated from Ranger school in April and was scheduled to report for duty in Korea in May. Susan flew up to Seattle to visit me before I was flown out. I doubt I was good company for her since I was recovering from some pretty significant stress from the rigors of Ranger school.

During my flight, I wrote her a letter, breaking off our engagement. Looking back, I can see it fit my pattern of ending things when they got too emotionally involved. Regardless, what a horrible way to end things.

As you can imagine, I broke her heart. She eventually shipped the engagement ring back to me and once I was back in the United States, I spoke with her over the phone and apologized for how I had handled things. It was a very awkward conversation.

Sometimes we become aware that the life path we are on is not right. It's an internal knowledge, a gut instinct that something isn't right. This is an opportune time to pump the brakes or push pause to evaluate where you are at. It's an opportunity to step back and reflect on the current situation. Why am I having the thoughts I'm having? Why am I feeling this way? Is there something I need to talk through with the other person? Do I have a coach, or trusted friend or advisor that I can use as a confidential sounding board to work through these thoughts and feelings? Can I role play it out?

Some people find it useful to journal their thoughts and feelings. Others use prayer or meditation to find clarity. Do you have a favorite place that you find serenity, such as out in nature? Where do you find peace, joy and clarity? Seek this place and sort through the challenging thoughts and emotions. Having an effective coach can also be very powerful when processing challenging situations.

Back when I was in the midst of that relationship, I knew not how to receive Susan's love. I had no understanding of what a gift she was to me and I had no idea that I would never experience that kind of love in my life again. Unfortunately, for both of us, I did not know how to accept her love nor did I have the capacity to love her in a manner she was worthy of receiving from me.

I think my self-esteem was too low to feel worthy of her love. I think the lack of love in my early life had prevented me from understanding or accepting love, so I drove her away. I was too insecure, too immature, and likely too afraid to accept what she so freely gave to me. I'm not talking about sexual intimacy (we were reserving that for marriage), but her open affection, deep consideration, and respect for me.

How do you receive love? Are you open to receiving? Are you aware when you are blocking or deflecting the love and affection of another? Sometimes we don't feel worthy. Sometimes the way in which our partner is trying to show, love doesn't match up with our love language. Showing and receiving appreciation are powerful aspects of love. Tuning in to to our partner to understand and notice all the good that they bring into our lives is important to recognize and acknowledge to the other.

Vulnerability and courage are needed both to receive and to share our thoughts and feelings. If we've not fully developed these capacities, there is always an opportunity to grow. We cannot change another person, but we can focus on our personal growth and rise up to elevate our partner or spouse. Our capacity to love another is in direct proportion to how well we love ourselves and the level of our own self-image. If we need to heal from something in the past, seek out help to emotionally process the past to show up in the present as our best self.

Our presence is the greatest gift that we have to give. Our capacity to show up fully with the thoughts and feelings within us and capable of effectively communicating while respecting our own boundaries and boundaries of the other is critical. This is a continuous journey we are all on. But we can get better each and every day with intentionality and consistency.

Committing to Love

When I returned from Korea, I landed in Seattle and drove across the country to report at the 82d Division Artillery (DIVARTY) headquarters at Fort Bragg, North Carolina. Following my paratrooper training there, I was assigned to C Battery, 1st Battalion 319th Airborne Field Artillery Regiment.

At the same time, I enrolled in a Business Administration Master's program, attending classes at night and on weekends. Throughout this time I developed new friendships with some outstanding young lieutenants in my battalion; these were some of the finest young leaders that I would ever have the privilege of serving with. On Saturday nights, we would often go to a local dance club, which is where I met my wife to be.

"Theresa" and I danced a few times and I worked up the nerve to ask her for her phone number and a kiss goodnight. That was pretty bold for me.

She lived a couple hours away so we alternated traveling to see each other for about a year. One weekend she brought her parents and younger sister along with her to Fayetteville. I invited a small group of my best buddies to join us for dinner at a local Japanese steak house but I warned each of the young lieutenants to be on their best behavior because this young lady was very important to me. They were, and they made a favorable impression upon her parents, who did not necessarily hold the military in high regard at that point. This helped my case as I was wooing their daughter.

I eventually proposed and she agreed on one condition: I would need to sign a prenuptial agreement first. That was fairly unusual back in the late 1980s and it was a little hard on my ego. It seemed like an affront to my motives; I was in love with this young woman but she would only move forward if I agreed to sign the document. I asked two members of the Army's legal staff (a husband and wife team of captains) to take a look at the document and provide me with some professional advice. They essentially told me that I would be giving up all my marital rights if I signed and advised against doing so.

I was young and in love and ultimately told myself that it didn't matter. I loved her; that was enough. Besides, I intended to be successful in my own right over time and that it shouldn't matter.

So we married.

My in-laws were always good to me and generous towards us as a young couple and our children as they grew into adolescents. But knowing that there was an underlying lack of trust remained in my subconscious. It was a cloud that remained over Theresa and me.

Love Co-Created

When Theresa told me that we were expecting our first child, she didn't receive the reaction she had hoped for. The word "pregnant" triggered the same fear I experienced the first time I'd heard those words; I'm sure it showed on my face. I actually was thrilled to become a father, but the shame from my past took center stage. It's somewhat hard to explain and possibly hard to understand but it cast a shadow over what should have been a joyful moment for us as expectant parents.

We attended Lamaze classes and read *What to Expect When You're Expecting* but soon discovered that no one is ever fully trained or prepared to be a parent to a precious young child. I knew one thing, however: I would show my son love and affection.

This commitment carried over to the next two children as well. All three boys were delivered in the same hospital in Memphis, Tennessee by the same OB-GYN and delivery nurse, who was a friend of ours. Each birth was a joyous occasion.

Throughout their childhood, I repeatedly told each of my sons that they were loved. I gave them verbal assurance and frequent hugs. Today, I continue to greet my grown sons with a handshake and a hug. And I always say "I love you" as we say our farewells.

I can recall rocking our first born, Conner, to sleep most every night; I think this gave he and I a strong bond from the start. I always hugged him and told him that I loved him before he'd head off to bed. To this day, there is always a warm embrace exchanged whenever we greet one another or wish each other farewell. He knows I love him, as evidenced by this excerpt from one of his college creative writing stories:

What Is a Story?
by Conner Howard

One of my favorite things I have ever been given was an old rag of a t-shirt that my father gave me at a young age. It was a shirt he had received in boot camp when he joined the army and he had had it ever since. I still have this shirt and love wearing it. For one, it was a gift from my father so I appreciate the sentimental nature of the present. It is also quite a comfy shirt being as weathered as it is. However, one thing I love about it is that it has an unknown history to it. It has a number of holes in it and one can't even read the word Army across the front because it is so faded, but that shirt has been on earth longer than I have been alive. It saw my dad at a young age and was a part of his experiences. I still know very little of my father and even less of his childhood and college years, but I love that I have this little piece of it. That I have this old faded shirt because there is a story to it and I want to know it. Really everything to me has a story and it is very difficult for me to narrow down exactly how to define it. If I would try though I would say that it is an appreciation of everything that is around us. Whether that be something real or fiction, it is an appreciation of the world and the interactions that take place in it. It is sharing of experiences and knowledge, which bind all of us together and allow for us to come even closer than we already are.

Conner still has the t-shirt; to him, "it's a thread that ties us together." Something else he adopted from me, he believes, is the importance of generosity. Kindness and the ability to help others are very important to him.

When he shared this, I smiled since it reflects my mantra for my real estate business: Helping Others Means Everything! Self-betterment and gift giving are important and fulfilling to him and I respect that. As Joseph Campbell once said, "The privilege of a lifetime is being who you are."

Our middle son, Cole, grew up strong with a tender heart and an engaging personality. I didn't always agree with some of his choices, but for my own peace of mind, I began allowing him to make many of his own decisions while he was in high school. Of course, I gave him my unsolicited advice about big decisions—such as accepting the opportunity to move up from junior varsity lacrosse to the varsity team a year early to help him reach his future goals—but in general, I refrained from letting him know what I was thinking until he asked.

As he has matured, I have continued to focus on letting him know I accept him and love him as he is. Are there things I might want for him that he hasn't yet pursued? Sure, but I can recall that when I was that age, I needed space to figure some things out on my own. It wasn't until later in life that I actively sought out support and guidance from my parents and other mentors.

When I asked Cole about what some of his best memories with me as a father were, he mentioned the many long-distance road trips we took for lacrosse tournaments and playing paintball together with friends in the woods. One of my fondest memories with him was when he and I completed the Wrightsville Beach, North Carolina triathlon together.

I was working away from home in Ohio managing an aluminum rolling mill at the time and he was supposed to fly up to spend a weekend with me but was unable to due to his first year at an academically challenging Division III college lacrosse program. I felt bad we wouldn't have a one-on-one weekend bonding experience like I'd already had with each of his brothers, so I challenged him to do the triathlon with me.

My goal was to try and beat his time, despite him being nineteen while I was fifty. He ended up beating me by a few minutes. I was proud of him and we have a great picture of us together in the transition area after the race—his arm around my shoulder—to commemorate the event.

Our youngest son, Clayton, was full of energy from day one. He seemed to be in perpetual motion when he was younger and quickly developed a great sense of humor and tremendous musical talents. I think it is natural for the youngest in a family to use humor as it can be a way to get more attention.

A couple of years ago he called to tell me he was participating in a retreat to help him in his relationships with others—and himself—and asked if he could read me a letter he'd written. It was a powerful moment that touched me deeply. It was courageous on his part to step out and try to connect with me on a level he never had done so previously; it was a blessing to me. I thought I'd share it here because it's important to understand that our perceptions can change about others in our lives. Sometimes we are unaware of how someone sees us. A useful thought I've gained in the last couple of years goes like this, "The thought or story I'm telling myself is…." We can have a thought and belief completely based on an inaccurate perception. Hopefully, we are all continuously open to growing. Sometimes we can have unexpected breakthroughs that significantly alter relationships in a healthy way. I hope this story can open possibilities to how a significant relationship in your life can change for the better.

Dear Dad,

Yesterday I started the Landmark Forum and it has made me rethink a lot of things. I came to the Forum thinking I wanted to work on my career. I wanted it to help me focus in on how to get involved in the music industry and feel confident about the direction I'm heading. A lot of things have come up though, like my lack of releasing music, my relationships with people and women and specifically my relationship to you.

I've never felt that we have had a bad relationship. We connected over many things over the years and have certainly had many good times. You definitely worked a lot and you have a work ethic I've always respected and admired. But I've always also felt that there was always something stopping me from getting closer to you. You are more reserved and less expressive than mom and I've always compared the relationships. With mom I've always been comfortable to say anything but I haven't felt that with you.

I've realized through the Forum that that was my decision. I think I chose this because it is easier. It's harder to have conversations about stuff that I thought you maybe might not agree or respect. As my dad I realize you'll respect anything I wanted to say because you love me. I want to talk about religion, politics, drugs, the divorce, parenting and so many other things. I love you dad and I know that you would have these conversations if I wanted to have them. So I think the new possibility I got from this is a better relationship with you by being honest and not afraid of your judgment. And also know I won't judge you. I love you and all I want is to be as close with you as I am with my other family members and friends.

Love,

Clayton

I think his underlying need was to know that I respect him—and hear me tell him so. Respect is so important, especially for men. Even though I'd worked hard at always demonstrating my affection to my sons and telling them I loved them, I still hadn't done enough to relay my respect for them.

How Love Can Be Shared

I'm going to share a story that ties each of the previous three together, since all three of my sons played the sport of lacrosse from middle school on. You may not have children. You may not be into sports. But you likely have a shared experience with family members. There are always ties that bind us. Sometimes they can be created by a singular event or sometimes from a series of events.

In this case, my sons' mother and I invested significant time and money to support their participation in a sport they loved to play with their friends. We loved to watch them and support them and encourage them.

It's amazing to me how many life lessons can arise out of what sometimes seems like things sports, clubs, associations, and events you get to be a part of. These lessons can have significant impact in shaping who we become and how we relate to others. Passion and suffering are common themes, both in love and in life. When we love, we truly will the good of the other. Sometimes we make tremendous sacrifice for those we love. In sports, this can be a teammate or a coach who mentors us. In families, it can be for the good of all or the unique special needs of a particular family member. We do things out of love. We carry forth the lessons.

When my boys were in high school, I started a tradition of giving a framed and matted print of a written work I created entitled, "Lacrosse Is About Life." It was presented to each of the graduating seniors for the four years my sons were playing varsity lacrosse at their school. I would get them matted and framed then get a name plate engraved for each graduating senior. The head coach would present the prints to them on Senior Day, usually the last home game of the season. Here are the words:

LACROSSE Is About LIFE

Lacrosse provides many lessons that will serve you well in Life. Lacrosse is not played by yourself and Life is not lived standing alone in the field of play. It's about teamwork, looking for the team-mate to make the extra pass to or slide to help when it is needed. Commitment. Caring for others. Love of the game. Love for Life.

LEARNING takes place from the time you pick up a stick and start to cradle a ball or do some 'wall work' bouncing and catching the ball. Different nuances are learned in how to catch, pass, or recover a ground ball. You learn new skills from coaches, practicing until you gain confidence in the newfound skill you've mastered.

ACCOUNTABILITY is developed by playing as a member of the team. It begins with getting in shape, playing hard on every play, getting your homework done and keeping your grades at their highest level. Your teammates are looking to you to make the play and your coaches reinforce this value, they are counting on you.

COMPASSION is experienced and gained when you, your teammate or competitor goes down on the field of play. You take a knee—hoping they are okay and we give applause when they are able to rise and walk to the sideline. You show compassion as victor shaking the hand of your competitor who played their best in defeat.

RESPECT is given and it is earned. You show respect to your coaches by following their instruction. You respect the rules by yielding to the calls of your referees. You earn the respect of your teammates by putting forth your best effort. You earn the respect of your opponents by executing your offense and defense well.

OPTIMISIM is contagious. Your coach, teammates, and fans cheer for you when you score, win a faceoff, or secure a ground ball. They are there with encouragement if a game is lost. Players with high motivation remain optimistic even when the score is against them. Your teammate's sense and feed off of your optimism.

SPORTSMANSHIP is displayed with a fist bump, or hand-shake to your opponent. It's helping your competitor up off the ground after a hard check or an inadvertent trip or fall. It's playing clean and fair when you are tempted to return a cheap shot. It's a congratulations to the winner whether it be to your or the other team.

SUCCESS in a game is measured by the results on the scoreboard. Success in life is measured in the content of your character. It is demonstrated on the field by how you play the game. Compassion, Accountability, Respect, and Enthusiasm are core to a character that will bring you success in life.

ENTHUSIASM is a force multiplier. It is demonstrated with your passion for excellence in practice, on the sideline cheering for your teammates, and the competitiveness you demonstrate in the game. It's the passion of a parent yelling encouragement from the sideline when you make a nice play. Show it—Be enthusiastic!

On the reverse side of each print, I attached this note:

LACROSSE Is About LIFE

These words came as inspiration
from watching my sons play a game they love
and the love a father has for his sons
seeing them strive to be their best on and off the field.

Tim Howard, Cape Fear Academy Parent
Conner '09, Cole '11, Clayton '12

When Circumstances Change

Following my release from the Army, I began a career in the aluminum industry which took my family from Memphis, Tennessee to Knoxville, Tennessee and then to Bettendorf, Iowa. Eventually my wife and I decided I would leave that career and we would start a franchise business in Wilmington, North Carolina.

Theresa and I enjoyed some good years before the boys were born and when they were young but eventually the strains of my extensive travel and too many roles requiring more and more responsibility took their toll. I simply did not invest in their lives at home like I should have; I was more focused on my career and achieving success at work than at home.

In addition, I don't think my wife or I ever figured out how to really meet each other's love languages. It's not that we didn't love one another at all; it's just that we didn't know how to do it as well as was needed. Our marriage ended, though not of my choosing, after twenty-nine years.

Sometimes things come to an end, not of our own choosing. Recognizing the ability to change in hard circumstances is key to carrying on and growing. Though the pain of the change may not be welcomed, it may be necessary to learn lessons that will serve you well later.

Questions to help you REFLECT The Life You Want™ when unexpected changes come about in life could include:

- How will I make the best of this unexpected change?

- What am I grateful for from this experience that I will carry forward with me?

- What do I imagine in the future that I can feel now that will be even greater than what I've experienced to this point?

- How do I take time to love and care for myself and show love to others as I am in the midst of this pain and suffering?

- What thoughts to I need to created to use as scripts to carry me forward to the next season in my life?

- Who can I rely upon to help me throught this change—my coach, mentor, respected friends, or family?

- What thoughts do I have about creating a new future, that fulfills the desires of my heart going forward?

We Are Conditioned for Love

Humans are wonderfully created beings. We enter this world full of joy and happiness, fundamentally understanding good and bad and fully dependent on our caregivers' attention. As we start to grow, we begin to be influenced and conditioned by our environment and family. If my lifetime of cause-and-effect experiences were recorded, it would look something like this:

As an infant, I'm happy when my mother holds me and rocks me. I'm upset when I need to be changed. When grandma and grandpa tickle me and make funny noises like "coochy, coochy," I laugh. I cry when I'm hungry until I am fed. Life is good.

I begin crawling and bump into the leg of a chair. It hurts so I learn to not do that again. I take my first steps; Mom and Dad sure are excited. I begin to fall down; mom catches me just before I hit the floor. I feel safe. A couple of hours later, I grab ahold of the coffee table to stand up; I slip. Mom and Dad are not there to catch me this time so I hit my forehead—ouch. I cry. Mom comes running; she picks me up and holds me. After a few minutes, I stop crying. Mom's soothing comments are reassuring; I feel loved and secure in my mother's arms.

As I get older, I begin to interact with others. Brothers, sisters, other kids at the public playground. There are other parents, too. An occasional dog. I am expanding my network of contacts and range of experiences.

I'm five years old and running in the living room. My older brother is chasing me so I slide underneath the coffee table. My ear lobe gets caught on the table and is cut. "Don't run in the house!" becomes a family rule that is programmed into my brain, along with "Chew with your mouth closed" and "Elbows off the table."

My parents now have expectations for me. In fifth grade I come home with a report card containing mostly B's instead of all A's. Seventh grade—a D in English. Whoooa; major dilemma. I've definitely let my parents down. Mom gives me "the speech" to get my act together. Will they love me more if I get straight A's? Will I feel any better about myself? I work hard to bring my grade up.

Freshman year in college. My English professor pulls me aside; he tells me he knows I'm better than the effort I'm putting forth. I feel a little ashamed and determine to do better.

We are thus conditioned by the words and actions (i.e., love) of others. Positive feedback, for example, is a powerful thing. When it is constructive (like that given by my college professor), we can take the information in, adapt, and improve. When others who love us and care for us give us insight into how we are impacting them, it can be useful. But oftentimes it is difficult in the moment to hear feedback. It is challenging for us to moderate our sense of self-esteem when we hear something that is directed at who we are. Our defense mechanisms tend to pop up. We react.

Some of us have a tendency to swallow it whole, or interject, all the feedback as if it is true about ourselves rather than just someone else's opinion. If our self-esteem is already low, this can have the effect of telling yourself, "See, you are _____ [whatever the person said]."

What Is Love?

Love is abundant. Free, total, faithful, fruitful. Love requires us to freely give of ourselves to others. It is unconditional. It does not place restrictions or limitations. It does not arise out of fear. It is eternal, everlasting. Our capacity to love others is endless.

Both Aristotle and Aquinas have talked about how to truly love someone means to will the good of the beloved, to look to the intention of love which has as its main objective the good or well-being of the other. The Italians have a beautiful little phrase they say that captures that intention. They say, "Ti voglio bene," which means, "I wish you good" or "I want what is good for you." Truly loving someone is looking outward towards one beloved and seeking what is best for them.

What does that all mean exactly? It means that you desire their good more than what you want for yourself. Take, for example, a parent with a crying baby in the middle of the night. The parent wants to sleep, but in their love for their little one, they get up to feed or change a diaper or simply comfort him.

To me, there is no greater gift in the world than being fully present with someone significance to you. To be fully alive and experience all your senses with them.

When someone fully commits themself to being with you in mind, body, and spirit—sharing all their thoughts, all their emotions—this is an honor and a gift.

Gift moments such as these are cherished, treasured, and loved—especially in today's culture when it's so easy to be distracted during our interactions with each other. Commit yourself to being fully present to those you care for. Whom you love and serve. Be transformed from within by this giving fully of yourself to the other, whether in friendship or in love or both. Being present—being fully you—will honor the other person and be a rich blessing to you and your heart.

Do you believe that you're loved as you are? Or do you feel like you have to please, perfect, prove, pretend, or produce in order to be loved and accepted?

Many of us, even those of us who grew up in healthy families, experienced some level of subconscious programming that told us we had to "prove" that we are worthy of love, whether it was from a parent, sibling, teacher, or coach. Even as adults we may work ourselves to death to achieve success not because we love what we are doing, but because there is an inner drive to "prove" to ourselves and others that we are worthy of love.

People I've worked with have said to me, "Maybe it's not the best motivation, but it's gotten me to the top!" That may be true, but wouldn't it be even better if you felt amazing along the journey to the top? What if you succeeded while also believing you are priceless, and knowing that yes, you 100 percent can and will go to the top. But *even if you don't, you are still good and worthy to be loved and admired.*

Ohhh, you felt that to your core didn't you? Perhaps you don't believe that's possible. Maybe you are afraid that if you lose that inner drive of needing to prove yourself, then somehow you won't be successful.

I get it; I've been there. But you know what I discovered? When I came to know my true identity and that I was worthy of love no matter what I did or didn't do, it gave me freedom. It was a new kind of freedom to soar to new heights, to be successful, *and* to fail forward without shame. Shame closes us up and will keep us stuck in some capacity.

The freedom to fail or succeed and be loved in the process is such a more joyful, peaceful experience than striving to get to the top because you're scared to death that someone will think you're not worthy of love. I've heard many speakers and coaches refer to that fear as "imposter syndrome."

"Love is not something we give or get; it is something that we nurture and grow, a connection that can only be cultivated between two people when it exists within each one of them–we can only love others as much as we love ourselves." –Brené Brown

"To be loved and not known is comforting but superficial. To be known and not loved is our greatest fear. But to be fully known and truly loved is, well, a lot like being loved by God. It is what we need more than anything. It liberates us from pretense, humbles us out of our self-righteousness, and fortifies us for any difficulty life can throw at us." The Meaning of Marriage: Facing the Complexities of Commitment with the Wisdom of God *by Timothy Keller.*

"For now we know love's secret, that to receive love it must be given with no thought of its return. To love for fulfillment, satisfaction, or pride is not love. Love is a gift on which no return is demanded. Now you know that to love unselfishly is its own reward. And even should love not be returned it is not lost, for love not reciprocated will flow back to you and soften and purify your heart." The Greatest Miracle in the World *by Og Mandino*

"If we all treated each other with the unconditional love as pets do, what a great place this would be." Tami Spaulding

Loving Ourselves

Somewhere along the way, many of us stunted our growth in the area of love, whether it was something we didn't freely receive in our family of origin or something that happened to disrupt our sense of loving ourselves.

When we love ourselves, we have a healthy self-esteem. It is balanced. We are aware of what we are feeling and what we are receiving from others. We have the capacity to love others within healthy relationships with appropriate boundaries.

We must learn to love ourselves, wholly and completely. Let's start right now! Scripts or affirmations are a powerful way to develop our capacity for love of ourselves and in turn others. They are positive statements we make about ourselves to ourselves to reinforce a belief we have and want to affirm.

First we need to stop saying, "That was stupid" or "I'm stupid." It breaks my heart to hear it. When we catch ourselves thinking poorly about a mistake we've made, what if we instead say, "I'm brilliant and I am able to learn from my mistakes." Every time you make a simple error, say to yourself: "I'm brilliant, and I am able to learn from my mistakes."

Let me give you an example. If I had said to myself *you're stupid* or *you're not a very good typist* every time I misspelled a word while writing this manuscript, I don't think I ever would have finished the book. Why? Because I'll bet I misspelled or mistyped at least one word per paragraph. (Remember typing papers with a typewriter and correction tape? Ah, computers with spellcheck are wonderful things!)

Another phrase we should remove from our internal dialogue is *I forgot.* What if we replaced it with "I remembered" instead? This is a concept I learned from my brother, Vince. When we do this, we are honoring a positive aspect of ourselves (gift of memory) rather than focusing on a negative (forgetfulness). It's a subtle yet powerful shift in our mindset that leads to more love in our self-talk.

As I mentioned previously, I don't remember a lot of love and affection freely given in my family while growing up. I know my parents loved me; they just didn't show a lot of physical affection. Each of them was challenged by their own family of origin so they did the best that they knew how to do as they raised my four brothers and me.

They certainly passed on some positive character traits: love of learning and knowledge, love of nature and the outdoors, love of music, faith, persistence, perseverance, and the ability to persuade. But it was not an environment with lots of nurturing.

Imagine a life without love; a life devoid of joy. What a miserable existence it would be. But where does love come from? What is its source? Love is from God. We are created with love and for love. Dr. Caroline Leaf writes that we are "wired for love."

This force, this power, this source of life loves us and provides within each of us the capacity to love ourselves. If we are created in the image of our Creator, then how could we not love ourselves? We are each designed and created to be loving beings. We are each designed to have the need for relationships with others.

But each of us has experienced love in different ways and therefore share it differently. My early experience of love was primarily shaped from a Catholic upbringing and later, from a Christian faith as an adult.

As I continue to develop as an adult, this presents challenges for me to be the type of husband and father I want to be. My sense of normalcy is based on my upbringing so when I glimpse other families' "normal"—open displays of affection, lots of laughter, and statements of positive reinforcement—I become uncomfortable and embarrassed. I have to learn behaviors that were not modeled strongly in my family of origin.

We are also to love ourselves. The capacity to give love is in direct proportion to our love of self. Sometimes there are serious issues that we need to work through to help us in our ability to do this. But we must. Life is meant to be abundant, full of love and joy. If we currently are not experiencing this, we have the power to change our lives.

We were designed to value our own life. We have instinctive mechanisms built into our neurological systems to protect and preserve life. Any being absent of love would not be programmed in this manner. Why would we value life but not love? It makes no sense. We need to work on feeling that love within ourselves regularly and abundantly.

Self-Worth

Our capacity to love is strongly influenced by our self-worth. What is self-worth? It is my own subjective opinion of my value as a person. It determines what I believe that I deserve. It affects our choices, our decisions, our behavior, and ultimately our future.

It's been said that we become the average of the five people we spend the most time with. When we are young, that's usually our parents, other caregivers, and siblings. As children, we don't have a choice in who we get to spend our time with, but as an adult, we may need to change who we're spending time with if we're feeling unworthy.

As babies, we learn our self-worth through what we'll call the 5 A's: acceptance, appreciation, acknowledgment, affirmation, and admiration. I like to also include affection! In our infancy, we are typically loved unconditionally.

By the age of seven or eight, that's when we start to become "conditioned" to achieve one or more of the 5 P's in order to feel loved: prove ourselves, be perfect, produce, please others, or perform. In the process, we can lose our sense of self-worth; our sense of being loved for who we are. We can lose our sense of dignity and self-worth when we begin to allow others' opinions of us to shape our own self-beliefs.

Our self-worth is based on a set of neural connections in our brain that are fired and wired according to our proving, perfecting, producing, pleasing, and performing in order to feel worthy or to feel loved. We develop habitual unconscious responses through repetition of behaviors.

Some major influencers of our sense of self-worth are our family, our environment, and our culture. In our families, sometimes we learn labels or criticism or comparison of others. We can learn to be appreciated—or not—based on our grades, our behaviors, and our performance in a sport activities valued by the family system. Our environment includes our friends, the schools we attend, and the communities we are a part of.

Whether we are hanging with the popular crowd for approval, performing for attention, or striving for accolades, we quickly become stuck in a cycle of constantly trying to do more and become better. We attempt to compensate for a sense of emptiness if our cup is not full of love and acceptance. Our culture can be brutal, particularly online. The influence of social media has had a significant negative impact on the self-worth of people who continuously compare themselves to others.

Good News

Since God is molding us to have the mind of Christ, and God is love, then we are being molded to have a mind filled with God's unconditional love. As Timothy Jennings, MD, explains in his book, *The God-Shaped Brain*, "Recent brain research by Dr. Newburg at the University of Pennsylvania has documented that all forms of contemplative meditation were associated with positive brain changes—but the greatest improvements occurred when participants meditate on a God of love. Such meditation was associated with growth in the prefrontal cortex (the part of the brain right behind the forehead where we reason, make judgments and experience God-like love and subsequent increased capacity for empathy, sympathy, compassion and altruism. But here's the most astonishing part. Not only does other-centered love increase when we worship a God of love, but sharp thinking and memory improve as well. In other words worshipping a God of love actually stimulates the brain to heal and grow."[9]

Dr. Caroline Leaf, in her book *Switch on Your Brain*, explained, "The scientific power of our mind to change the brain is called epigenetics and spiritually it is as a man thinks so is he (Prov. 23:7). The way the brain changes as a result of mental activity is scientifically called neuroplasticity, and spiritually, it is the renewing of the mind (Rom. 12:2.)" 1

In one of her podcasts, Dr. Caroline Leaf talks about how the brain has a natural bias toward optimism—how we are what she calls "wired for love." This means that when we are connected to others in deep and meaningful ways, and when we are satisfied with where we are in life and where we are going. Even during the ups and downs of life, which will always remain a constant in our lives, we can function at a healthy level. The brain likes it when we are in a good place!

---

9.   Page 27, InterVarsity Press, 2013.

Dr. Masaru Emoto, a scientist and water researcher, has revealed how thoughts and vibrations affect the molecular structure of water. Through high-speed photography of thousands of water crystals, Dr. Emoto has shown that the most beautiful crystals are formed after the water is exposed to the words "love and gratitude."

Even science shows how *love* (which is actually Someone—i.e., God!) is the most life-changing force in the world.

Dr. Caroline Leaf says, "Our genetic makeup fluctuates by the minute based on what we are thinking and choosing... You control your genes; your genes do not control you. Genes may determine physical characteristics but not psychological phenomena. On the contrary, our genes are constantly being remodeled in response to life experiences...

Our choices become physiology, and what we believe as well as what we believe about ourselves alters the facts. We are not victims of our biology. We are co-creators of our destiny alongside God."[10]

Thus, according to Dr. Leaf, our self-perception can be improved by epigenetics (our free will in regard to our character and conduct) and neuroplasticity, thereby allowing us to wire and rewire our brain by the choices we make.

"Neuroplasticity can operate for us as well as against us, because whatever we think about the most will grow—this applies both to the positive and negative ends of the spectrum," she says.[11]

Take the Gold and Leave the Dirt

During a meeting discussing various directions for this book, Maria and I talked about the idea that in most things there is something good to be learned even if there are other ideologies we may not buy into. Maria termed this idea as learning to "take the gold and leave the dirt" whenever we are learning something new, whether that is through reading a book, listening to a podcast, or hearing a talk.

---

10.   p. 50-53, *Switch on Your Brain.*

11.   p. 63

Many times, people (myself included) throw the baby out with the bathwater. When there's some information, concepts, or beliefs I disagree with, I tend to disregard it all and walk away rather than ask myself, *What can I learn? What if I'm wrong?* Simply asking those questions could lead to a beautiful new discovery.

As I've done my own internal growth and work of healing and wholeness, I have found that when I'm becoming defensive or writing someone or something off, I need to pause and do a little praying and journaling about why I'm feeling that way. What can I learn from this person or situation or talk or book? Is there some truth in it? Can I take the truthful concepts and apply it to my life or use it to fuel goodness in the world? Are there some other ways to view this? As I continue to develop this habit, I am finding so much fruit in the gold!

When we dismiss new or different ideas, we actually do a disservice to ourselves and to the God who made us because He gave us brains to examine things thoroughly. Rather than merely react, let's choose to explore our thoughts and emotions. Too often we are being given a gift but because we don't like the wrapping paper, we toss the whole thing out before we even see what's inside.

Keeping the gold and ditching the dirt is a skill set that can be learned. It is a beautiful opportunity to step into deeper intimacy with the Lord by allowing Him to guide us in truth and discovery.

MARIA'S VIEW

Some people only associate love with pain. "If that's what love is, I don't want it!" they say. I could be wrong, but I think when we believe that "love is only pain" or "love isn't worth it," we aren't actually looking at what love is, but rather at what was missing. Let me explain; a parent losing a child to death—it hurts so badly because they loved that child so deeply and now that child is gone. Yet, every parent I've met who has loved a child and lost them to death has said they would do it all over again even as painful as it was; loving that child was the biggest gift in their life.

"To love at all is to be vulnerable. Love anything and your heart will be wrung and possibly broken. If you want to make sure of keeping it intact you must give it to no one, not even an animal. Wrap it carefully round with hobbies and little luxuries; avoid all entanglements. Lock it up safe in the casket or coffin of your selfishness. But in that casket, safe, dark, motionless, airless, it will change. It will not be broken; it will become unbreakable, impenetrable, irredeemable. To love is to be vulnerable."-- C.S. Lewis from The Four Loves

When I think about the most painful seasons of my life, and I think about why they were so painful, I can identify it's because I loved deeply and yet, maybe the love wasn't reciprocated, or maybe things didn't turn out the way I had hoped or expected…In reality, it wasn't the love that hurt, but rather the absence or lack or brokenness of it.

Several years ago I went through a heart-wrenching breakup from a serious relationship. Less than a month later, my music teacher, Ed, who was such a gift in my life, was murdered. A few weeks after that, my family endured a painfully tragic event and on its heels, my cousin died unexpectedly. I don't have the words to adequately describe that kind of heart devastation.

I didn't know it was possible to have one's heart broken to such an extent, or to cry that many tears. So. Much. Sadness. But why so much sadness? Because there had equally been So. Much. Love.

If I could go back and erase those people from my life because of the pain associated with their losses, would I do that? No, I wouldn't; because the gift of the time spent, the gift of each person—those don't change just because they're not here anymore or because the circumstances changed. The lessons I learned from them and the precious life-changing moments we shared—those changed me. They made me into the person I am today. Which brings me to forgiveness.

I don't believe we can love ourselves—or anyone for that matter—without including forgiveness in that equation. During the immediate aftermath of so much tragedy, I found myself not being able to respond and act the way I normally did. I inwardly berated myself for not handling everything better and constantly apologized to my housemates for not being my normal, joyful self. One of them finally pulled me aside and kindly said, "Maria, you got hit with so much recently. I don't expect you to be happy all the time, or to say the 'right things' or to be jolly all the time. Why do you expect that of yourself? Can you give yourself some mercy, grace and love? Can you be kind and patient with yourself?"

Her words hit me like a ton of bricks. Why *was* I expecting so much of myself when I was in such a broken, dark place? To get it "right"—whatever that meant in those situations—by behaving and showing up a certain way rather than giving myself grace to have "off" days as I processed all that had happened. I felt that if others did something kind for me, I had to make sure that it was repaid rather than simply receive it. My housemate's questions allowed me to forgive myself for my imperfect ways of handling a challenging season and started me on the path to love and see myself more how God does. It also brought me into the process of forgiving all of those people associated with those losses.

Grief impacts each of us differently, it does interesting things in our hearts, minds, and lives. I remember saying, "If I didn't love this person so much, I wouldn't care so much and it wouldn't hurt so bad!"

But would I really want to be the kind of person who doesn't love? Would I really want to be the kind of person who is so worried about getting hurt that I lock my heart up, as C. S. Lewis says, so that my heart becomes impenetrable and unbreakable?

One day during that tragic time, I was sitting with the Lord, tears just streaming down my face, and I told Him, "Jesus! My heart is ruined! It's completely broken! It can't be fixed or put back together!" And all of a sudden, an image of my heart—burst open, blood flowing all over—popped into my mind and I felt the Lord say gently, "My Maria, your heart is broken, but here's the thing; I don't put broken hearts back together because a heart that is broken is a heart that is open and as the blood flows in and out it's actually life blood---and that open heart will in reality enable you to both love *and* be loved so much more!"

I realize you may not have a relationship with the Lord or understand some of the things I'm saying. I'm not here to preach to you; I can only share my experiences. No matter what you believe spiritually, the fact is that love makes us vulnerable. Love requires us to be both good givers and good receivers. Love requires risk. It means there's a good chance that our hearts will ache. It doesn't matter whether it is love with God, or a family member, or a friend, or a significant other—to love at all is to be vulnerable and to be open. But love is always worth it.

Our Sense of Beauty and Being Loved

"You are the most beautiful girl in the world!" "Son, I am so proud of you!" Every time I hear a father or mother tell their little daughter or son that, it brings a certain joy to my heart.

Our first understanding of who we are—our self-image—begins at a very young age and is primarily bestowed on us by our first caregivers (usually our parents). Knowing our worth and how to view ourselves, as well as love ourselves is based on the ways our caregivers know and love us.

But what if such loving affirmation and affection was withheld from us? What if while growing up there was some perceived need to pretend, be perfect, or perform well in order to be loved? Those things can negatively shape our self-image and the way we love or don't love ourselves. I find that the majority of people, even those who had great parents, feel the need to prove their worth to some extent and lack a full measure of self-love.

While I wouldn't say I ever doubted I was loved, it's interesting how much, at least for girls, our worth ties in with whether we feel we are beautiful or not and how that correlates to being loved.

Raised in a Catholic-Italian family, I was the second oldest of six kids and, as previously mentioned, the only girl. My brothers were very athletic and adventurous and I held the belief that I had to be as good as them at everything they did. It didn't matter that girls weren't usually very good at football; I was going to be the exception.

When I played sports or participated in outdoor adventures with my brothers and their friends (who also became my friends), I felt loved and accepted. I could hold my own and I felt confident and special.

It was a different story when I went to dance. As much as I enjoyed the rough and tumble, I adored putting on a pretty costume and *loved* dancing delicately on my toes for hours on end. But this was when I first encountered the cattiness of other girls.

My ballet teacher never said anything when I came in for rehearsal with Band-Aids showing through my pretty pink tights—a result of having played roller hockey, ramping, or climbing trees earlier that day.

But suddenly, I realized I didn't fit in. And I wanted to. So I entered the unspoken, ongoing battle to be the skinniest, have the most beautiful make-up, be the teacher's pet, and be a part of the "cool" dance group.

As time went on, I continued to dance as well as play sports and be outdoorsy and adventurous, but I began to doubt my attractiveness. I would think, *maybe I'm just not pretty. Maybe I need to be skinnier.* In middle school I remember hearing the girls talking in the dressing room about being "anorexic." I didn't know exactly what it was, but I gathered it meant being skinny. So for a brief stint I started praying that I would become anorexic. Praise God that prayer was not answered in my life!

When my parents and brothers noticed I wasn't eating much, they called me out by telling me I was too skinny. Thankfully, I valued their opinions and determined to maintain a healthy weight, regardless of what the other girls said. I'm so grateful that health was a focus in our family rather than having to look a certain way when it came to healthy habits regarding food or working out.

The thought *I must not be pretty* did not go away, however. Eventually, I resigned myself to it and decided it was okay. *If I can't be pretty like the other girls then I'm going to be really good at everything I do and I'm going to have a great personality.* Holding on to that thought, I dove into life. If you can't beat them, join them! I intentionally began calling out the good and beautiful things I noticed about others around me.

It wasn't until I was in my early twenties when a memory of middle school popped into my head, of when I first thought I wasn't pretty. For whatever reason, I started bawling. I drove to the nearest Catholic Church and sat in a pew with Jesus, asking Him three things: Show me my beauty and worth, show me how You see me, and show me who You are as my Father.

Every day for the next year I sat with the Lord and asked those same three questions, writing down what I felt He was telling me. Unbeknownst to me during that time, the repetition of the Lord speaking into me about my worth, my beauty, and who I was as His daughter rewired my brain. That year shifted everything. It was literally life changing as I started walking more and more into my God given identity as His beloved daughter.

Even now, as I look back on that season of coming to know who I was as His beloved, I see how incredibly important and vital that was for me to know my worth and identity as beloved daughter in the depth of my heart and soul. That deep inner "knowing" gave me the freedom to live life with arms wide open, excited about the possibilities of what could be, because knowing you're loved– *period*, not for what you do, or accomplish, or whether you get something right or not. To know one's worth—to know that it can't be earned but rather that it's given—*that* is priceless. It's freedom. And that is the truth of our reality as beloved sons and daughters of the Father.

Maybe you're reading this right now and the story you've been told and that you continue to tell yourself is that you're a mistake, you're a screw up, you have no worth or value, you're not loved and you don't matter. Maybe the story is you have to earn your worth or earn being loved. I could stand here all day and tell you repeatedly that none of that is true, that you do have value and worth because it was God given from the beginning and no one can take that from you. But I know from working both in coaching and ministry that it's not that easy.

So instead, I want to invite you to take a minute, close your eyes, take a few slow, deep breaths and pray that prayer with me: "Father, show me my beauty and worth, show me how You see me, and show me who You are as my Father." Then sit in that space, imagining God the Father looking at you tenderly. What thoughts come to mind? What do you feel in your body? Just that awareness can be helpful.

I want to invite you to begin to do that everyday and just see what changes. Don't give up if you don't feel anything different after a few weeks. It literally took me a year of doing that everyday before I felt a massive shift. I'm not saying it will take that long, but what I am saying is that every person I've encouraged to do this has felt a shift eventually in the way they see and feel about themselves. So go on, try it! I dare you!

Long Lasting Love

I've always loved a good love story. I particularly admire elderly couples who demonstrate that they are still deeply in love with each other. At weddings, my focus, more often than not, is on the grandparents of the newlyweds more than the just-married couple. Why? Because I can tell from watching the older couples that they *know* what love is and how to live it out.

During college I waited tables at a steakhouse and especially enjoyed serving the older couples. I could tell from watching them that they shared a deep, rich history, and love for one another. I typically asked about their story: How did you meet? What did you first notice about one another? What are three things you attribute to having a beautiful, loving marriage?

After doing this for years, I noticed that they all shared similar responses: trust, communication, praying together, having fun together/laughter, and asking themselves every day, "How can I make his/her life better today?"

When I think about those things, it strikes me that those intentional actions are the recipe for true, genuine, vulnerable, life-giving, and long-lasting love.

I dated someone briefly who told me that I never really seemed to open up and share my feelings. At the time, I was confused and thought to myself, *what else do you want me to open up or share about?* It wasn't until years later that I understood what he meant and began sharing from a place of openness and vulnerability. To be super honest, I'm still learning how to do that. Although it can be scary and a life-long process, it is one of the most important and rewarding skill sets we can learn in relationships.

Brené Brown says vulnerability is "uncertainty, risk and emotional exposure." She also says that vulnerability is the birthplace of love, belonging, joy, courage, empathy, and creativity.

Ironically, the one thing we are all made for and which we crave is to be truly seen, known, and loved. It is also the one thing that we are all petrified to do. In order to fully love others and be loved in return, we have to enter into vulnerability. This means we have to let ourselves be seen and received in all of our glory *and* in all of our mess. That can be a simultaneously terrifying and liberating process. But as Brené points out, we should only share our authentic story with those we deem worthy of hearing it. This means we don't have to be vulnerable with everyone, but with those who have the right to our story.

I believe vulnerability, which can create a place for deep love, is a two-fold skill set. On the one hand, sharing openly allows you to courageously break down your own barriers. On the other hand, it creates a place for others to also bravely open up.

How do you create and hold that space for others? One of the best ways is to come from an internal place of curiosity rather than judgment. When someone shares something personal it can be a scary thing for them; there is fear of being judged, of being shamed, being thought less of somehow. Few things shut a person down quicker than shame and judgment. However, in being curious (the word "curious" actually comes from the root word in Greek meaning "to care") and drawing one out with love and care, in seeking to understand rather than condemn, *that* is a powerful healing force when someone shares with a person who is asking out of genuine love and care.

I'll be the first to say that I am a massive work in progress when it comes to some of these skills. But the beautiful thing is the more we have self awareness of where we are in this process, the more we can be intentional in the actions we want to choose to take, rather than our normal default.

Many times there are things hidden in our lives that need to be brought to the surface in order to be healed. It's so interesting how our various relationships can bring things up in our minds, hearts, and lives that we would prefer to remain hidden because it's a sore spot or perhaps because it can cause conflict. Yet that's the beauty of relationships. They bring those things out in us because we have a Father who wants us to be healed and whole and we can't be healed if we keep shoving things down. At some point, whatever we have been stuffing or avoiding will erupt and show itself in our lives. The game changer is when we recognize it's something that God wants to use to heal us rather than destroy us. But we must be brave enough to walk through the pain into healing.

One really powerful prayer that I have prayed with my significant other is "Lord, please give us Your awareness, self-awareness, each-other awareness, and other awareness."

We have found that the more we are aware of who our Father is, the more we know who we are. And the more we know who we are, the more we can give ourselves to each other and those around us *and* the more we can receive each other and those around us—all in a selfless love. It's been a beautiful source of healing, growth, and an increase in love.

Everything matters. If there's one thing I've learned over the last few years, it's that not a single part of our story is wasted. Each moment, each season, every heartache, joy, tears, laughter, challenge, new experiences, mistakes, growth, people we encounter—all of it prepares us for the next moment in life; the next season.

I think living with intentionality and love is really about leaning into the moment you're in while you're in it, not being so concentrated on what's up ahead or dwelling so much on the past that you miss where you are right now. It's learning to embrace your reality while still working towards your hopes, goals, and dreams of the future.

I'm blown away when I look at the "randomness" of my life—the wide range of experiences, travels, people, challenges, pain, joys, heartaches, laughter, and so much more. I can confidently say that *God does not waste anything* that happens in our lives.

Everything works together for our good. Everything matters, even the smallest details. Everything comes into play. Life happens *for* us, not *to* us. But are we looking for it? If not, we'll miss all the beauty and intricacies that mark the fingerprints of a Father who truly cares about every single hair on our head and every single detail of our lives.

Looking in the Mirror

You deserve to be in spaces and relationships that contribute to who you are created to be, that feed your soul, and help you to grow. You are worthy of connections that are loving, nourishing, kind, and authentic. So before you settle for anything "less than," remind yourself that the places you visit and the people you journey through life with, do they support you and contribute to your sense of feeling secure, loved, and enough? (Now re-read this paragraph aloud and substitute "I/my" for "You/your." Claim it for yourself.)

JOURNAL EXERCISES

Who are the people in your life that truly love and support you and encourage you to be your absolute best self?

_____

_____

_____

_____

Do you love yourself?

_____

_____

_____

_____

What were you taught about love growing up?

_____

_____

_____

_____

What are your current thoughts and experiences around love in general or self-love?

_____

_____

_____

_____

What do you want to do and think differently about love going forward?

_____

_____

_____

_____

Who is someone in your life you want to love better?

_____

_____

_____

_____

What thoughts do you need to shift in order to put that person's good above your own?

_____

_____

_____

_____

How do you want to love well going forward?

_____

_____

_____

_____

CHAPTER 5

"Whatever is noble, whatever is right, whatever is pure, whatever is lovely, whatever is admirable—if anything is excellent or praiseworthy—think about such things." —Philippians 4:8

"It is not the mountain we conquer but ourselves." —Edmund Hillary

---

Energize your thoughts towards that which you intend to be.

TIM'S VIEW

I sat ashamed, embarrassed, and humbled in the company commander's office at Camp Darby, Georgia near the end of my U.S. Army Ranger training. I had been informed I would not graduate with my class; instead, I was given the option of being recycled through another two weeks in the Florida "Swamp" phase or quit and go home.

I had come from a long family line of military men: My father, maternal grandfather, two uncles, and a cousin had served in the Army and another uncle in the Navy—all during wartime eras. Although they didn't try to sway me to join the military, I nevertheless found myself following in their footsteps during my college years when the ROTC program offered the structure and responsibility I needed to help me focus on my studies and graduate.

It was during my ROTC years that I was introduced to the Army Ranger element and discovered my leadership skills. I enjoyed the camaraderie and training in ROTC more than school and soon decided that the military would be my career.

With that goal in mind, I attended both the U.S. Army Airborne ("Jump") School at Fort Benning, Georgia and Northern Warfare Training in Alaska the summer between my sophomore and junior years at college. I earned my airborne wings without incident but wasn't able to complete the Alaskan training due to a fall from a rock face that chipped a bone in my left foot.

On the ride to see the doctor, I saw one of the coolest sites I'd ever seen: Thousands of huge salmon swimming upstream to spawn. The scene was a gift moment to offset the pain of my injury that resulted in a cast and crutches for a few weeks.

The next two years were challenging physically, especially during ROTC road marches and extensive running, but I endured the pain and pressed on to reach my military career goal.

At the close of my senior year at Gonzaga University, I was named as a distinguished military graduate and became a commissioned second lieutenant in the U.S. Army. I then completed a short duty assignment as an ROTC battalion training officer at Fort Lewis, Washington before driving to the sweltering heat of Fort Sill, Oklahoma, home of the U.S. Army Field Artillery School.

I had two primary goals when arriving at Fort Sill. First, do my best and learn as much as I could in my Field Artillery Officer Basic Course (FAOBC). Second, earn a slot at Ranger school. I achieved both goals, which initiated a legacy process for myself.

I didn't know anyone in my class when I started the basic course, but I quickly became friends with Royd Lutz, who had attended the United States Military Academy at West Point. Royd had a more friendly manner towards me and the other ROTC graduates than many of his West Point peers. Nevertheless, Royd had a quiet toughness about him in spite of his outwardly friendly nature.

I was a little intimidated by the West Point graduates, truth be told. The competition to get into any of the service academies is tough; only the brightest, best athletes and potential leaders are selected from across the country to attend these demanding and challenging institutions.

Royd, like me, was not overly impressive physically—no one would have pegged us as future Rangers based on our appearance. I was six feet and weighed 165 pounds; Royd was five-eight and about 142 pounds soaking wet. Therefore, we decided to participate in the Ranger PT (Physical Training) rather than the normal PT with the rest of our class. Ranger PT was led by a couple of Ranger-qualified army captains who were attending their advanced course at the artillery school and would be the primary judges of who would receive a coveted Ranger school slot.

Despite our intense workouts, Royd and I realized early on that if getting a slot for Ranger school was based purely on who had the highest PT score *above* the perfect 300 standard score, then we were at a distinct disadvantage. However, Royd and I were both in the top 10 of the class based on our overall FAOBC scores by that point. Since we believed our primary purpose for attending FAOBC was to learn to be a proficient Field Artillery officer, which included much more than just pushups and running, we developed a proposal that included not only standards for physical fitness, but also our core artillery school performance, day-and-night land navigation courses, knot-tying proficiency, a timed twelve-mile road march with weighted rucksacks, and some field training/patrolling exercises.

After presenting the plan to our Ranger PT leaders—they had to buy into the idea first because they would be the ones coordinating and evaluating all these additional activities on top of their already busy schedules—we were given the opportunity to present it to the Field Artillery school student battalion commander, a lieutenant colonel. He adopted it pretty much as we put forth and variations of it have continued to be used over the years.

I graduated with honors as one of the top seven students of the artillery school and finished second overall in artillery fire direction gunnery skills. But for me, the greatest accomplishment of all was hearing my name called out as a recipient of one of the limited slots to Ranger school ... and Royd got one, too.

This is an example of energizing your thoughts towards that which you intend to be. Both Royd and I were intentional and persistent in going after something we believed in. We put forth the extra effort to excel in the curriculum while developing a new process that would enable us an opportunity to compete for something that meant a great deal to us both. We never lost sight of our goal to attend Ranger school and we stayed focused on achieving this while also achieving our primary purpose of completing the artillery school.

Have you ever had a big dream? Set a really big goal? It takes a powerful "why" to keep you going when once you get underway and you encounter adversity. Because you will face adversity. Are you in touch with your "why?" That's what will keep you moving forward with the discipline to succeed when the inevitable challenges arise.

It is important to take time to reflect upon this and it's worth taking the time to journal about. Get crystal clear with yourself about what is driving you. What will motivate you to get up every morning to get to the gym or do a daily prayer, meditation, or gratitude practice? What mindset do you need to develop to keep moving forward towards your goals and dreams?

Previous chapters spoke about gratitude and recognizing how you feel as you imagine accomplishing your goals. Build upon these principles as you begin to energize your thoughts towards the person you intend to become.

And So It Begins

I reported to Class 4-85 of Ranger school at Fort Benning, Georgia for the winter session of the patrolling phase. The first week of school is officially called the Ranger Assessment Phase (RAP), which (by design) tests the students' physical fitness, endurance, and some basic field skills such as hand-to-hand combat and combat water life-saving. We Ranger candidates, however, referred to it as "City Week." Training days usually start at approximately four o'clock in the morning and last until around midnight. All training events are back to back, allowing minimal or no time for rest and recovery.

Upon meeting the non-commissioned officer in charge of the school (who was friends with the retired sergeant major back at Gonzaga University), I was assigned as the executive officer, or XO, of the Ranger Training Company during the entire patrolling phase.

What that meant for me and my Ranger buddy was enduring twice as much physical pain and harassment than the other 200 Ranger candidates. Because we had to arrive early to receive instructions about the day's activities from the Ranger Instructors (RIs), we were forced to do all sorts of physical fitness activities until the rest of the company arrived—lots of pushups, deep-knee bends with the full weight of our rucksacks, inverted pushups with our feet elevated on a tree, burpees, and so forth. When we got to the point we couldn't do anymore ("smoked"), they got us on our feet and gave us instructions right before the company arrived.

After I relayed the instructions to the Ranger candidate company commander, we then "fell in" to get smoked all over again with the rest of the company. It was brutal. I felt bad for my Ranger buddy, who eventually dropped out after a week or so. He was the first of many; I cycled through several Ranger buddies.

Once my company and I completed the patrolling phase, we moved on to Camp Merrill in Dahlonega, Georgia for the mountain phase. Two memories stand out in my mind.

First was a night that the lightning storm was so bad we put all of our weapons and radios at the base of a tree and stepped back so we wouldn't get struck. In the process, a tree branch hit me in the eye.

The second memory was when I lost all the feelings in my hands due to cold-weather exposure and I got written up for wearing polypropylene glove liners.

The mountain phase was where I had to say farewell, for a time, to my friend Royd. He had suffered a cut on his right hand that became infected and turned into cellulitis, causing his hand to blow up like it was a latex glove balloon. He was sent back to Fort Benning for a week of medical care and recovery.

The rest of the class and I moved on to the desert phase at White Sands Missile Base in New Mexico, not far from El Paso, Texas. By then we'd lost a significant portion of our class, either due to injuries, like Royd, or candidates simply dropping from the rolls voluntarily.

A very small portion of Army enlisted and officer candidates even attempt Ranger school, probably about 1 percent. The graduation rates of Ranger school have historically been about 50 percent or less, including the recycled students. About a third of students get recycled at least once during the training before completing. My hunch is by the end of mountain phase, we'd probably lost a third or more of our class.

Have you ever quit anything? Have you ever felt as if you had failed at something? I've learned that I only truly fail if I give up trying. As long as I keep moving forward towards my goal or developing the kind of person I intend to be, I cannot fail. So I've developed a mindset to get into action and stay in action: Fail, forward, fast (or, as I prefer, fall forward fast). If I fall down, I pick myself back up and keep moving towards my goal or developing the skill that I want to refine.

In the Rangers, we have a motto—Rangers Lead The Way. It came about during World War II ahead of the attack on Omaha Beach on D-Day. It's a mindset that I adopted and have stuck with ever since. It's not just that I strive to be my best, or to accomplish something before others; it's about being brave and stepping out with courage to face new experiences, to try things I've not accomplished before, to set an example for others. So I energize my thoughts with this underlying mindset to guide me and keep me moving forward.

Pressing On

The desert phase was where some of my biggest challenges began. Somewhere along the way I'd developed a really bad case of pinworms, which resulted in lost training time as I was taken back to base for treatment. Then there was the constant battle of sleep deprivation and malnourishment.

A Ranger student's diet and sleep are strictly controlled by the RIs. During time in garrison, students are given one to three meals a day, but forced to eat extremely quickly and without any talking. During field exercises, Ranger students are given two MREs (Meal, Ready-to-Eat) per day, but are not allowed to eat them until given permission.

This is enforced most harshly in patrolling and mountain phases. The two MREs are generally eaten within three hours of each other, one post mission, and the other prior to the planning portion of the mission. Though the daily caloric intake of 2200 calories would be more than enough for the average person, Ranger students are under such physical stress that this amount is insufficient.

One day I found an old pound cake in a slightly corroded C-ration can in the desert. Because food was a precious and limited commodity during training, I stuck it in my rucksack and surreptitiously ate it later that day.

Sleep was also elusive during this time. It seemed like every time we would finally be allowed to get some rest, we'd get hit by the opposing forces and have to move from our patrol base on towards our next objective. For the better part of a week, no one got much of any sleep at all in the platoon. After the course was completed, I calculated I averaged about an hour of sleep per day during those eight weeks of training.

On top of all this, I periodically experienced a health challenge that affected my abilities as the navigator or pace-count man during my platoon's movement. One night we were making our way across the desert when I lost my eyesight. Everything just went dark. I called out to the Ranger instructor to let him know that I was alert, but I could not see; he shut down our movement right there for some rest. I was embarrassed, but it wasn't anything I had any physical control over. For the next two weeks, usually once a day, I'd lose my eyesight for a period of time, forcing me to tie off to my Ranger buddy with a six-foot rope and carabiner.

We all face obstacles in life. How we respond to these challenges speaks to the character that we have been able to develop. Much of this flows from the thoughts we have in our minds when faced with adversity. Creating a strong mindset is a skill that is developed and reinforced with regular daily habits. My co-author, Maria, shared a gift once with me with the following writing:

Watch your thoughts, they become Words.

Watch your Words, they become Actions.

Watch your Actions, they become Habits.

Watch your Habits, they become your Character.

Watch your Character, it becomes your Destiny.

What have you done to develop your thoughts and daily habits towards designing the life you want to create? Are you prepared for the setbacks that will surely come?

"Within every adversity is the seed of an equal or greater benefit"
– Napoleon Hill

There's Always a First Time

The flight from El Paso, Texas to Camp Rudder at Eglin Air Force Base in the panhandle of Florida gave us all a chance to finally get some much-needed shuteye before parachuting into the conclusion of our training—the swamp phase. This was only my second experience with in-flight rigging and also proved to be my first experience using my reserve parachute.

The moment you step out of the aircraft is always one of the most exhilarating—you get the "prop blast" or "jet blast" in your face and experience the sensation of falling for approximately four seconds. You also have the relief of getting out of a very crowded and often hot aircraft. On that jump into Florida, however, those welcome experiences were short lived and quickly replaced with the utter terror of realizing there was a partial malfunction of my parachute.

In Airborne training, you're taught to exit the aircraft in a particular position with your chin in your chest, leaning slightly forward, and your feet and knees together. As you fall, you count to four, then look up to check your canopy. Well, on this occasion, I couldn't look up because my risers (the webbing connecting my parachute harness to the suspension lines of the parachute) were all twisted up into what is known as a "cigar roll."

For a full or total malfunction, you just pull the ripcord on your reserve. With a partial malfunction, you are taught to put your left hand over the front your reserve parachute and hold it, then pull the ripcord with your right hand while keeping your left hand in place. You then dig your right hand into the reserve pack, pull the reserve parachute out with both hands, and throw it out down and away below your feet and in the direction of your spin. This gets drilled into you over and over and over in airborne training until it becomes a force of habit when an airborne instructor calls out "Hit it!"

The one thing they don't explain and can't simulate is the high velocity of your spinning in this situation. I'm not sure what elevation we jumped out of the aircraft, likely 1,000 feet above ground level or so, but I finally got my reserve chute fully deployed fairly close to the ground. I landed coming down through a scrub oak tree and got my suspension lines all tangled up in its branches. I laid on the ground for a moment, thanking God that I was alive, that I hadn't broken both my legs, and that I was still able to continue my training. I eventually had to cut some of the suspension lines of the parachute to free it from the tree branches.

Once we all made it to the barracks, we showered for the first time in more than a week. The really disturbing thing was seeing ourselves in the mirror for the first time since Ranger training began. Most of us looked pretty rough. I had lost nearly thirty pounds in less than seven weeks; I could see all my ribs and my face had sunken cheeks. We all looked fairly emaciated.

Perhaps because of that, the Ranger instructors allowed us a rare treat that first night—all the care packages that had been sent to us throughout training were finally distributed and everyone shared what they'd received. Stale cookies never tasted so good! My fiancée had mailed a love note with an Andes thin mint ironed flat between wax paper so it got through as a non-contraband letter. It was a chocolate mint I will never forget! We also had the opportunity to read letters from family and loved ones and sleep in an Army bunk again—for one night.

The training in Florida was some of the most intense we experienced. We navigated cold-water swamps, built rope bridges, and crossed the Santa Rosa Sound for a waterborne assault from Zodiac-type boats. We also completed our first live-fire assault courses with rifles, machine guns, grenades, mortars, claymores, and so forth. When your team or squad members are all suffering from severe sleep deprivation, it gets a little spooky as you hear real bullets buzzing by your head.

An airmobile mission with UH-60 Blackhawks also caused a rush of adrenaline. I had rappelled off plenty of rock faces and training platforms in the past, but never from a helicopter. I'm fairly tall at six feet, so trying to stand up in a Blackhawk with a large, heavy rucksack on my back was challenging. The RI eventually had me sit down and he pushed me to get going.

Unfortunately, instead of descending feet first as I was rigged for in my rope harness, I fell headfirst. With the carabiner and rope configured for a standard rappel, there was no friction for deceleration. All I had was the strength of my hands gripping the rope as I descended rapidly, upside down. My hands felt painfully hot from the friction. I literally bounced off the ground head first; thankfully, my Kevlar helmet did its job. When I sat up and pulled my gloves off, I discovered second-degree burns across both sets of my fingers and palms. I spent the remaining time completing the swamp phase with blistered hands.

With only days left to complete the course, I blacked out as we were walking through the woods one night, falling face first into the sandy dirt. As one of the RIs was slapping me on the face, I resumed consciousness and came out swinging. Fortunately, I didn't make any contact with the RI. The next morning, as we were loading out for an airmobile exercise, I experienced severe dizzy spells that included nauseousness and having difficulty standing up. I didn't know at the time how sick I was. I had been persevering through so many different challenges.

I ended up going to sick bay for twenty-four hours while the company continued training. I felt horrible. I wasn't healthy, but I felt worse about not being with my platoon and helping my fellow Rangers. This event, combined with my previous incidents, pushed me into the category of missing too much training time to graduate. Thus, after the bus ride back from Eglin Air Force Base to Fort Benning, Georgia, I landed in the company commander's office and learned I could quit and get a letter forwarded to my unit commander and into my official military record that I was a leadership failure or I could be recycled through the entire Florida phase.

It was a humiliating moment. I felt like I'd let myself down, let my peers down, and let the Army down, for that matter. I chose to be recycled. I was down, but I wasn't quitting after all that I'd been through. I wasn't going to abandon my goal of earning the coveted Ranger Tab.

Most of us have had a goal or desire that wasn't realized. Depending on how long we prepared for it or held the desire in our heart and mind, the level of disappointment can vary; sometimes it can seem devastating. But we are in control of our response. Our thoughts are optional. How we face such unexpected challenges reflects our current mindset, skill set, and depth of meaning.

Recycled and Recalibrated

For about a week, all the other recycled students and I were stuck in a barracks together and given various demeaning duties. I was also sent to the Army Hospital to get checked out. A full series of lab tests showed that my liver and kidney functions were off the charts. After ruling out hepatitis, it was determined that the slightly rusty pound cake I ate in the desert had done more harm than good to my body. I was given some medication and released for training. The great thing about heading back to Florida was being reunited with Royd, who had recovered from his infection, made it through the desert phase, and was now ready to complete the swamp phase with me.

When you are recycled in Ranger school, it's an interesting dichotomy. To some you are practically scorned because you didn't make it through the first time. To others, you are highly valued because you know what is likely coming up next in training.

I took it upon myself to volunteer for the tougher assignments within the platoon. The few days I had back at Benning to recover with some sleep and full meals made a huge difference in my mental psyche and physical well-being. I still wasn't well, but I was suffering less and remained highly skilled at land navigation and pace counting. I took on the rotation of carrying the M-60 machine gun or radio when our squad was not on point. This was in addition to my rucksack that weighed 60-80 pounds, which was about half my body weight at the time. Royd described the process of donning the rucksack as a "turtle roll"—laying down on top of the sack, reaching your arms through its straps, and then rolling over onto your knees before standing up.

I successfully completed my second round of the swamp phase and thereby completed Ranger school. Royd also graduated and at the ceremony, his mom pinned our Ranger Tabs on to our uniforms. We not only achieved the goal we had set for ourselves back at Fort Sill, Oklahoma, we also developed a new evaluation process for the Field Artillery School that would carry on in the years ahead. And most of all, we had accomplished something together that on our own, never would've been possible.

I attended Royd's wedding the weekend after we graduated and then flew back to Seattle. Mom and Dad picked me up at the airport and were startled to see the obvious physical changes in me. Glad to be home, I slept for the better part of the next three days.

Mission accomplished.

Energizing Your Thoughts

As my story has shown, you *do* have the power to change your life. This power begins with a thought. You either accept this as truth or question it. Regardless, you are thinking about it—right now.

I ask you to accept it. Agree with it. Start to energize your thoughts towards what you want in life. What type of person do you want to be? What kind of relationships do you want to have? What type of work do you want to do? How will you fulfill your God-given purpose and honor the gifts he's given you? What financial success do you want to have? What do you want to achieve? Whatever it is, you have the ability to create it, beginning with the thoughts in your mind.

It has been scientifically proven that each thought in your brain creates an activity that can be measured. Electroencephalography (EEG) is the methodology that neuroscientists use to understand and measure brainwaves. A vibration at a specific frequency is created in your mind. There are different levels of brain frequency activity such as beta, theta, delta and alpha frequencies. (See research studies for more details on brainwave frequency if you have interest.) Your thoughts emanate within you and pass through you out into the universe. As Henry Ford said, "Whether you think you can or you can't, you are right." You see, you have the power to change.

When *you* start to believe that you are something different, that is when you will start to become who you want to be. Your current state is a reflection of previous thoughts, beliefs you've had, goals you've set or not set, things you intended to do or not do. These all bring you to where you are right now!

> **Change begins with a thought and is followed by energizing action.**

What was the energy that it took to complete the U.S. Army Ranger school early in my life as a young second lieutenant? What causes a person to push themselves beyond what their body is capable of doing to complete a task that their mind tells them they must do? These are interesting questions I've posed to myself, which you might be wondering about as well.

For me, in the past, achieving a particular goal resulted in a sense of satisfaction or accomplishment. I often made a commitment to do something I felt was needed to help me move forward personally or professionally. Rock climbing, rappelling, or skydiving, for instance, caused me to confront my fears and place trust in others or equipment. Completing my first triathlon was to prove to myself that I could do it and also to help me to get in better physical condition. Taking Latin dance lessons forces me to be vulnerable and humble, yet leads to increased confidence and joy from the dancing itself. As I have matured in life, I've learned to focus as much on the person I'm becoming as the goal or summit I'm working towards. My internal peace, joy and contentment are worthy objectives.

What motivates you to achieve a goal will be distinctly personal to you.

Need for Validation

When I was in my twenties, I constantly strove to achieve greater goals. I thought if I accomplished the goals, I would feel better about myself. Yet even after achieving them, I still felt empty.

Once I recognized this, I began to reflect on why I felt this way, which led me to incorporate a family of origin study as part of my Master's degree coursework. The time spent interviewing my parents and some siblings about their experience growing up and discussing our family experiences together helped me identify a want within myself that led to self-destructive thoughts and behavior.

I discovered that the single greatest desire I sought was validation; the desire to feel loved simply for who I was. I wasn't yet completely aware that I was actually looking to be able to love *myself* and accept *myself* just as I was. So I sought validation and acceptance in work by accepting tougher and more significant projects, hoping for recognition, promotion, and greater financial reward. I sought validation by serving others within my local church and in my city by building homes with Habitat for Humanity. I sought validation in relationships through an appreciation of my knowledge and service, which held the danger of personalizing what should remain professional.

At the root of this need, I think, was my unfulfilled desire for my parents to openly express their love and acceptance of me as a child. It led to a vicious cycle of disappointment, emptiness, and guilt.

What I eventually learned, however, was that I needed to replace those negative emotions with gratitude. Gratefulness comes from a place of no expectation. You recognize your blessings and engage a spirit of thankfulness, which births a desire to give rather than receive.

MARIA'S VIEW

I still have cassette tapes I recorded when I was about six years old that feature me singing and playing the piano. I began formal piano lessons when I was eight and I subsequently dove right into all things music. Because I wanted to become a professional singer and musician who got to travel and record albums, I spent hours playing and singing in our music room. And years later, I achieved my music dream. Almost all of it.

A big part of my background is being a musician. I took piano lessons for many years and while I learned a variety of different genres none of the teachers I took from taught jazz. One day, I decided I needed to learn jazz. I felt like there was more in the music world and my lack of understanding the 'jazz tools' was holding me back musically speaking. Enter in Ed. He was the most incredible teacher and while unconventional, he knew how to put those tools to good use and to teach me how to do the same. "Maria, all I'm doing is giving you tools to be able to pull out of your toolbox whenever you want. I'm also teaching you the rules so you can break them. All of this is going to give you a whole new level of creativity and freedom when you play!"

And it did! The crazy thing was as a musician I always had those tools at my fingertips; but I had never been taught how to use them to bring such beauty, freedom and creativity in my writing and playing until then.

I had always wanted to learn how to play jazz but it seemed like the one genre that was out of my reach since there never seemed to be any jazz musicians where I lived. Nevertheless, after traveling for several years, I decided to inquire once more at the local music store. The man working the front desk shook his head. "Sorry Maria. Unless you want to go to Nashville…." he paused for a moment. "Actually, on second thought, there's a guy named Ed Dansereau who's an unbelievable piano player and teacher. I think he may be teaching here in Bowling Green now. He's a little unconventional, but he's really good and he knows his stuff."

Unconventional or not, as long as he could give me the tools I needed to expand my playing—and wasn't creepy—I was okay with a little "different." I took his number and promptly scheduled my first lesson.

My first impression of Ed was that he seemed nice enough, but definitely had a bit of a gruffness about him. (I later came to see that his gruffness covered an incredibly soft, generous heart). He asked me to play a few scales and songs so he could see what I could do. Then I asked him to play for *me*; I wanted to see what he had to offer and what I could learn. His talent was unbelievable. Unconventional or not, this man knew how to play a piano backward and forward, up and down and in every key. But could he teach?

In the music world, someone is typically either a performer or a teacher, but not usually both. Ed, however, was a rare bird. He could do it all.

He opened up a musical world for me that I had never before experienced. He taught me the rules so I could break them (musically speaking), how to put together licks, music theory, and how to piece them all together. Many times as I watched his fingers fly over the keyboard and listened closely to the notes, I would sigh, feeling a little hopeless.

"Ed, will I ever be able to play like you?"

"No, Maria. You will be *better* than me. You'll have your special style, but you'll be better."

His belief in me, coupled with an inner determination to succeed and to show him that his belief in me and my music skills were not ill placed, motivated me to work hard. There were times I would go out to my car and cry from the frustration of not being where I wanted and from Ed pushing so hard, but I understood he was pushing because he believed in me.

As I worked, I began moving forward at a pace I never could have imagined and began playing things I had only dreamt about. Ed had that rare gift of convincing his students to believe in themselves and as his student, my own belief intensified through practical application. He saw what I couldn't yet see. I learned to borrow his belief.

Ed's life changed mine. And to this day, I am so grateful for who he was and the skills he taught me, but also for his belief in me. I was devastated when his life was cut short all too soon when he was murdered. But the gift he gave me during our time together is something that I'm able to keep on giving; just as sound waves continually bounce and stay in the universe, the notes he played and taught me to play will live on forever.

In thinking about this idea of "energizing our thoughts," I'm convinced that belief plays a large part. When I first started with Ed, I *thought* I could learn, but that belief wasn't in my heart. Ed, however, believed with his whole person that I had the capacity to learn and excel and that he could teach me how to do it. By working with Ed, the belief in my head little by little transferred to my heart.

We all need someone to believe in us. Even if it's just that one person who sees the potential in us and knows it can be maximized. That's the value of having a teacher or a coach or a mentor, isn't it? Or even a good friend or a family member who can call out the good, the gift, the potential, and encourage the work it takes to achieve.

Our thoughts are energized as belief is actualized.

Faith Over Fear

Would you say you're afraid of something? Fear is such an interesting topic and it comes up a lot in coaching. I've had many clients share that they are afraid of not being smart enough, not having what it takes to succeed, being "too much" or "not enough." Some people describe their entire personality as fearful. But is that true? Is fear just a part of life we have to accept or do we have any say in the matter?

I once read a *Smithsonian Magazine* article that explained how fear may be as old as the earth in that it's a deeply wired, fundamental reaction that has evolved to protect organisms from perceived threats to their existence. What's fascinating is some of the main neurochemicals involved in that "fight or flight" response are also some of the same ones involved in happiness, excitement, and other positive mental states.

I've heard many athletes, performers, and speakers share how they were scared to death before going out on the field or on stage until they decided to shift their focus from being "fearful" to being "excited." The body reacts the same way, but the focus is totally different. If you're focusing on being excited rather than scared, you're going to show up differently. For example, many times we end up self-sabotaging ourselves and our dreams by focusing on what could go wrong rather than focusing on what could go right.

The following Native American story beautifully underscores this point.

"A big fight is going on inside of me," an elderly Cherokee says to his grandson. "It is a terrible fight between two wolves. One is evil; he is anger, envy, regret, sorry, greed, arrogance, guilt, self-pity, resentment, lies, inferiority, false pride, superiority, and ego. The other is good; he is joy, love, peace, hope, humility, serenity, kindness, generosity, empathy, truth, faith, and compassion. That same fight is going on inside you and inside every other person also."

The grandson thinks about this for a moment before asking his grandfather, "Which wolf will win?"

The grandfather replies, "The one you feed."

We give power to what we focus on. If we keep thinking about how scary something is, that becomes all we can see. Fear lowers our immune system, raises our stress levels, and greatly diminishes the quality of our lives. When we live in fear, we stop living and we become selfish.

But the beautiful thing is we get to choose whether we let fear or faith win in our lives. We get to choose what we let "energize" our thoughts. Scripture says, "Perfect love casts out fear."[12] Something I have learned to do when I'm fearful about something I know would actually be good to step into is to pause, take several slow deep breaths through my nose and out my mouth, and then decide, "Okay! I'm going to do this!"

Keep in mind that there is a short window of time—five seconds, to be exact—that exists between the moment we have an internal instinct to change and our minds killing that idea. Therefore, speaker and author Mel Robbins encourages people to do one simple thing when they're afraid to move forward in their next step in business, whether it's making phone calls, writing a book, or having a hard conversation. She recommends that when you feel hesitant before doing something you know what you should do, countdown "5-4-3-2-1-GO!" and move towards the action.

---

12.   1 John 4:18

Ways to Energize Our Thoughts

"I am created for...." How would you fill in this blank? What are your dreams and goals?

Our imagination can be unlimited! We are made in the image and likeness of God; we are designed to create and imagine. We do so effortlessly as children and yet, at some point in our lives we're usually told to stop; that we need to get our heads out of the clouds and "grow up" or "be realistic."

But if we want to be intentional about creating a beautiful life, then relearning to use our imaginations is going to be paramount!

When focusing on clarifying your goals, here are some thoughts to consider: You are a gift in who you are and you have specific things that you bring to this world in a specific way that no one else can. Do you know what you're created for? In our chapter on love, we talked about being created from love, for love and to love, all of which is true. Now, in thinking about that, how can you shape your life in a way that helps you dive into what God created you for?

Or maybe you're wondering how you can develop clarity around that call or mission. The best way in conjunction with prayer is imagining; we create in our minds first! Everything begins with our thoughts.

Think about it: before we had light bulbs, someone thought about it. Before we had planes that flew in the sky so effortlessly, it was first a thought. Before anyone ran a five-minute mile, someone first thought and believed it to be possible.

Are you defining yourself by your past limitations or are you focused on the possibility of what could be? When we define ourselves by our past, we often limit ourselves to our previous failures and limitations rather than pushing forward towards a God-size vision and dream.

We can develop skills to more effectively energize our thoughts. We can increase our capacity to be firmly decisive. We can increase our mental capacity for resilience. We become what we think about. What we visually imagine is what we create in our lives. Our ability to create is a function of our imagination; this is our true intelligence.

"Imagination is more important than knowledge. Knowledge is limited. Imagination encircles the world."—Albert Einstein

It's never too late to learn these skills. You, with the Lord, are capable of creating a compelling future for yourself. You can design your life intentionally; you get to consciously decide. You have a God-given autonomy and freedom to choose to think and feel and act and create.

Freedom is a funny thing, though; it can be a double-sided coin. I've always said that we rise and fall based on what we think about and believe to be true about ourselves and about who God is. Essentially, we take this freedom we've been given and shape our lives with the thoughts of what we believe we deserve. If we know our worth and value as beloved sons and daughters of the Father, this can be an amazing thing. However, if we don't know our worth and how loved we are, then we can find ourselves thinking so poorly about ourselves that rather than reaching up towards potential and exploring the gifts, dream, and mission He has given us, we can find ourselves at the mercy of our self-deprecating thoughts and self-sabotaging the good things we were created for.

We need to get very, very intentional with our imagination and visualization. These are powerful tools that are meant to be used wisely. In order to design our lives with the Lord, we need to invite Him into the imagining and visualizing process of our minds, then watch how those thoughts become flesh in our lives.

We also need to practice intentionality. If we are consistent and apply intentionality to our goals, we will be amazed at the way they materialize. Our focus needs to be on designing our future with our imagination. Neurologically, we want to increase our skill set to wire and rewire what we are created for. It's about claiming what we think about—what we desire!

Our self-worth (what we believe about ourselves) greatly impacts what we go after in life or whether we even believe it's possible. If we don't believe we're worthwhile, or have a point for being here, then chances are, we're not going to think the kind of thoughts that energize us to take action and go after any dreams, or anything that would require much energy or effort, because, well, what's the point, right? But if we know our worth that was bestowed on us by God at the moment of our conception—if we recognize how valuable and loved we are—that makes all the difference.

So begin by being aware of what you actually think and believe about yourself or what you're wanting to learn or do. Invite the Father into that space to help you see and know how loved you are and how you do have the capacity to learn and do. Then work on repetition of thoughts. For example, if you want to believe you have what it takes to build a business, you could write down daily, "I have what it takes to learn how to build a successful business." Or, "I am learning more everyday how to build a successful business."

Belief and thoughts are only part of the equation, though. You've also gotta take action! If you want to build a successful business, what are the skills you need? What kind of training? Dive into those!

Each of us is in charge of directing our thoughts towards our desired ends. We can create new empowering thoughts that move us from the general to the specific. An important first step is reevaluating what we are created for and our self-worth. We are worthy of acceptance, appreciation, and a positive environment, whether that is at our home or work.

What we allow ourselves to aspire to is up to us. You can decide, "I'm thinking bigger!" You can develop new scripts for yourself, related to your profession, such as:

I deserve to find work that I love, and I look forward to doing.
I deserve to be at peace.
I deserve to be respected.
I deserve to be loved.
I am designing my dreams.
I am a man/woman of vision.
I have a strong imagination.
I am capable of imagining.

As we imagine, we go through a process of progressive realization. The friends we choose are critical! For instance, in friendship we become like the five people we spend the most time with. This was a concept that Jim Rohn first introduced many years ago.

Growing up I always remember my parents talking about how 'you become like the people you hang with.' And it's so true! We all want and need companionship along our life journey and who accompanies us on this journey matters and greatly impacts us, whether we realize it or not. For example, if you're around people who complain regularly, don't believe anything is possible beyond their current reality, and thus don't take any action steps towards a better life, then it's likely you will find yourself following in those same shoes.

This doesn't mean you can't have friends or family or others in your life who think or act differently than you. What it does mean is the people you keep closest to you are the ones you will subconsciously emulate. Remember, we all need help to bring our dreams and goals to fruition and to become the best version of ourselves. If your closest friends are not helping in that endeavor, then you may want to rethink how close you want to be with them or how much time you want to spend with them. One of the best pieces of advice I've received was to "make sure you're surrounding yourself with people whose values, integrity and example you want to follow or you will find yourself lowering your standards to fit in with those around you."

Which of your current friendships are helping you become who you want to be? It's important to be selective about who helps us to build our unique contribution to society. In turn, we want to be a supportive friend. This requires that we be very intentional about how we listen, how we inspire, and how we share. We want to value people's trust, protect their private conversations, and honor their vulnerability. We each need to be clear in our individual roles.

All of this flourishes under high standards and appropriate boundaries, and requires effective communication, intentional collaboration, and consistent actions.

Newton's Third Law of Motion As It Applies to Our Thoughts

Newton's third law states that for every action (force) in nature there is an equal and opposite reaction. In other words, if object A exerts force on object B, then object B also exerts an equal force on object A. The third law can be used to explain the generation of lift by a wing and the production of thrust by a jet engine.

How does this apply to our thoughts? Our current thinking is wired into our past thoughts, stored in our subconscious mind. We need to intentionally focus on new thinking that supports the direction we want to go.

If we are going to design and create a different life for ourselves, it will require change. It will require us to take different kinds of actions, or more consistent actions than we are already taking in our life. These actions will flow from the thoughts we repeatedly have in our minds.

For instance, if I want to improve my self-worth, I need to start having different thoughts in my mind. A script can be repeated over and over again until it becomes a belief that we accept about ourselves. For example, if I don't feel loved, I could start with this script to change my mindset and begin to create a new sense of self-worth: "I am loved. I am accepted. I love and accept myself as I am working to become the person I want to be".

I can simultaneously make improvements to my health and fitness when I make a physical change that supports the mental shift. For instance, if I lose weight and feel better about myself, it'll be easier for me to receive the script I am rewiring into my thoughts. If I'm feeling healthier, I likely will have more energy, and I may sleep better. All of this will contribute to a better physical state that sets me up for a more positive mindset that I bring with me into the world each day.

"Whatever we plant in our subconscious mind and nourish with repetition and emotion will one day become reality." –Earl Nightingale

So take action to create new thoughts. The thoughts that you have up to this very moment are optional. You have total control of what you are thinking. So if you want to have a new thought, make the decision to do so. Start rewiring your thinking to a better thought and reinforce it with repetition until it becomes a new way of thinking for yourself.

Scripting, which some people refer to as affirmations, is a power force to energize your thoughts towards that which you intend to become. You will likely run into resistance within your own mind when you begin, but be steadfast. Stick with it.

Different scientific studies have shown different lengths of time it requires to rewire our thoughts and to create new habits. Give yourself a chance for success. Start with repeating a script every day for 3-4 weeks until it starts to feel like you are beginning to believe it within yourself, then keep repeating it for 2-3 months until it becomes what you are. Once you've mastered this new mindset in this area, select another thought that you'd like to improve. Use the same "force" of scripts to develop the new thought and rewire a new belief about something else.

Attitude

One of the most powerful forces we have is our attitude. The attitude we project to others is the attitude they will reflect back to us. This is a key mirror principle. We want to be projecting a positive attitude so that what reflects back to us is, in turn, positive. Even though it may challenge the direction we have begun to move, it will create space for effective dialogue about the changes we are making for ourselves. The good news is that we can exert a huge amount of influence on how others treat us based on the attitude we project to them. It's like an echo—the attitude we put out will come back to us!

We determine the way people treat us. Give them the respect they deserve and they will open doors for you. Give people the benefit of the doubt. Always focus on projecting a positive attitude regardless of what someone else may be doing. We never know what struggles they may be facing at the time and we may be the one bright light in their life that they get to experience when they encounter us. When we reflect a good attitude to others, we can start to see a shift in their response.

In recent years we've heard a lot about Emotional Intelligence, or EQ, in the workplace. The first element of EQ is our self-awareness. We want to be aware of the attitude we are projecting onto others.

As Earl Nightingale once said, "We all want good results from life, in our home, in our work, and in all our contacts with other people. The *most important single factor* that guarantees good results, day in, day out, all the months and years of our lives, is a healthy *attitude*! Attitude is the magic word."[13]

We want to radiate a "can do" spirit and positive energy. It is palpable when someone walks in a room with an extremely positive attitude. We all sense it, and are impacted by it immediately; the room feels different. It is so powerful that it affects all of those around us.

With a positive attitude, we reflect a spirit of love and carry within us an energy force. It is constantly impacting the world around us. We are either bringing life or robbing life with those we encounter. It is ultimately our choice. Awareness is the key that unlocks our ability to choose. Our attitude is the lens in which we see and steer our lives towards our eternal destiny. It is the secret ingredient to life.

> *"Nothing can stop the man with the right mental attitude*
> *from achieving his goal. Nothing on earth can help the man*
> *with the wrong mental attitude." –Thomas Jefferson*

Our attitude is the composite of our thoughts, feelings, and actions. Whatever you focus on becomes your reality. Therefore, a person with a powerfully positive attitude is always focused on things like possibilities, service, achievement, success, and going the extra mile. His attitude becomes a potential source of generosity to every person he meets. As a result, one man's attitude can change the world. He can either bury it or give life with it—only he has the power to choose.

---

13. *The Strangest Secret*

We each have the ability to choose our thoughts (intellectually), which in turn become our feelings (emotionally), which then motivates our actions and causes the world around us to react to our actions. By consciously directing our thoughts, we can be a powerful force for good. Awareness of our attitude enables us to make the best choices for our lives.

"Attitude is the reflection of a person. What's happening on the inside shows on the outside. Our attitude is incalculably powerful. It can bring about marvelous results for us. But we must train it patiently, day by day." –Bob Proctor

Attitude is also an energy that we project to the world. Our energy, based on our attitude, creates our reality. We spoke earlier about Newton's Law of Cause and Effect; if we put these concepts into a mathematical formula, it would look like this:

Thoughts + Feelings = Action (Energy) → Attitude (Force)

"The last of human freedom—the ability to choose one's attitude in any given circumstances." –Viktor E. Frankl

Viktor Frankl survived a Nazi concentration camp with the control of his mind. In the midst of horrible circumstances, he held onto the overarching goal to survive in order to tell others, so that no one else would ever have to experience it again. He taught us how powerful our mind can be; that in spite of whatever we face, we have the ability to choose our thoughts. He used his mind to energize his thoughts to escape from the camp and go on to teach the lessons he learned and impact so many others lives in a positive way. Can you imagine enduring such circumstances and coming through with such a positive outlook?

Here is a question to ask yourself: Does my current attitude repel or invite the life, the people, the environment, and impact that I want for the world?

We want to become aware of the thoughts in our minds. The thoughts we are having now is what will come forth in our lives. Our words paint images in our brains that cause thought patterns. If you were to assess the thoughts in your mind, would they contribute to a positive attitude?

Our attitudes have been neurologically wired and through neuroplasticity, we can change our thoughts. Neuroplasticity is the capacity of our brain's neurons and neural networks in the brain to change their connections and behavior in response to new information, sensory stimulation, development, damage, or dysfunction. We therefore want to learn to become intentional about using this capacity to rewire our neural connections in a way that helps us become who we want to be.

This recent breakthrough in neuroscience about neuroplasticity puts aside the old theory that the brain is fully formed early in our development and then remains static for the rest of life.

Now we know that everything we do alters our brain not only on the molecular and cellular level, but also leads to the rewiring of the brain. When we learn, walk around a new place, meet somebody new, or achieve a new experience, our brain and its connections change.

We can leverage this understanding to develop new mindsets for ourselves.

Key Steps to Change Your Attitude

1 - Become aware of how you are showing up. If your external environment is negative, reflect on your internal environment.

What thoughts are you having about yourself? How does that manifest in your surroundings? Is your home and workspace well organized? Or could it be more tidy?

2 - Take responsibility for your own attitude.

Are you blaming others for your circumstances? Or are you taking ownership?

3 - Forgive your past self—you are not that same person anymore.

Have you forgiven yourself? Are you carrying shame or guilt from the past? What do you need to let go of to be your best self?

4 - Decide to lead yourself first by changing your habitual thoughts.

Take control of your thoughts. Develop scripts for yourself that support the self-mage you want to create for yourself. Utilize "I Am" statements of who you intend to become.

5 - Change your thought patterns.

Are you ruminating about the past or are you living your best in the present? Are you imagining the life you want to create for yourself or are you focused on what you could have done differently in the past?

Key Focus Areas for a Positive Attitude

1 - Be a person of hope. Always find ways to encourage, bless, and inspire others.

If you have a positive outlook, you will radiate this with others that you encounter. Be a light for others and an example for others to follow.

2 - Focus on gratitude, abundance thinking, and thanksgiving.

If you focus on what you are lacking, you will get more of what you don't have. Be grateful for the blessings that already exist in your life. The more grateful you are, the more grateful you will become. So see the good, and you will notice even more good that already exists.

3 - Be a person of responsibility, make no excuses, keep your commitments, and don't blame others.

You really only have control over one person—yourself. So take full responsibility for who you are and how you show up. If you don't like the person you currently are, then become a better version of yourself. It may take a while for your circumstances to change, but how you respond to the current situation is totally within your control.

As you can see, our attitudes have a powerful impact on the direction of our life. When we energize our thoughts in a positive way towards our future self, we will begin moving in the direction of our dreams.

Let's now shift to gaining clarity within ourselves. Can you see yourself clearly? Can you identify what it is you are grateful for? Can you identify the emotions you feel inside? Do you have the self-awareness or emotional intelligence to clearly articulate your wants and desires? Let's do this by completing a vision exercise to create greater internal clarity:

In the columns below, or on a separate sheet of paper or journal, write down something you like about yourself on the left. Then on the right, write the emotion you feel about yourself when you think about this trait. Do this for at least three things.

I Like About Myself:		Feeling:
I am able to run three miles	:	I feel healthy and fit
I read regularly before I go to sleep	:	I am grateful to learn new things each night
	:	
	:	
	:	
	:	

Going through this exercise may also have brought up ideas about things you want to change or improve or a different set of circumstances you want to create for yourself. To move these thoughts into outcomes, you need to clearly focus on the outcome you want for your life.

"*Without vision the people will perish.*" –*King Solomon,*
the richest man who ever lived Proverbs 29:18a (KJV)

You can change your life. You've seen that there are things in your life that you are grateful for. Yet there may be a desire for something beyond your current circumstances. If you are focused on your present set of circumstances, this is where you will remain unless you move your thoughts to what you aspire to become.

See yourself as you want to be: no doubt, no fear, and confident. *Feel* the emotion that is present within you as you visualize what you will become or achieve. This is your personal vision.

Write it down, stating clearly what it is you want. Make it realistic for yourself. What is something that you can begin today to move you in the direction that you want your life to become? If you have big dreams, start small and build upon successes. For example, do you want a wonderful loving relationship with your spouse? See it in your mind to begin the process to create it. Your imagination will help to get excited about your dreams. Your emotions that flow from these thoughts will help you to get into action towards your goals and dreams.

For instance, if you want to run a marathon, but never have, imagine the feeling of accomplishing this goal. Start by walking a comfortable distance. Progress to jogging at a comfortable pace. Get a marathon training guide with a progression that makes sense for you, your work and family life, age and current level of fitness. Track your progress as you improve as this alone will help keep you motivated towards your goal. Sign up for a race so you have a hard-and-fast date to prepare for. Get an accountability partner, maybe someone to run with or someone to check in with each day. These are concrete ways that you can move from an idea, into actions, and ultimately achieve a goal.

Looking in the Mirror

Are your thoughts currently energized towards the future and becoming the person you desire to be? How's your attitude right now? Does it need a little shifting? We hope that you will make an honest thought reconnaissance of your current inner thoughts and discover your current patterns. With this self-awareness you can begin to shift your thinking towards thoughts that will serve you as you pursue your dreams.

JOURNAL EXERCISES

What is something you're passionate about? Is there also a need for this? How can you reduce pain in the world?

_____

_____

_____

_____

What seems to come naturally to you?

_____

_____

_____

_____

What is something you would want to do regardless of the level of income it provides?

_____

_____

_____

_____

What is something you can do or create that you think people are willing to purchase? Is there a value for this product or service?

_____

_____

_____

_____

State in the present tense what you will have accomplished through your energized thoughts. What would you say to yourself?

(e.g., "I am so happy and grateful now that...")

_____

_____

_____

_____

Here is a powerful exercise to plant affirmations in your mind and help them take root, blossom, and grow:

1. Write the affirmation (e.g., "I *am* courageous!").

2. Read it *out loud*, running your finger underneath it as though you're just learning to read. That helps to wire it in your brain.

3. Set your timer for anywhere between two to ten minutes and visualize what you wrote down. If you're saying "I *am* courageous," what would that feel like? What would it look like? How would you experience it in your body, your heart? Try to see it in your mind and feel it in your emotions. Imagine a scenario where you are practicing courage.

4. Do this exercise once a day minimum. For greater impact and results, do it in the morning, afternoon, and evening.

Affirmation #1

_____

_____

_____

_____

Affirmation #2

_____

_____

_____

_____

Affirmation #3

_____

_____

_____

_____

CHAPTER 6

*"A friend loves at all times and a brother is born for a
time of adversity."—**Proverbs 17:17***

*"You are the average of the five people you spend the most time with." — **Jim Rohn***

Clarify your inner circle.

TIM'S VIEW

I had recently been promoted to be the executive officer (XO) of a Field Artillery firing battery of the 319th Airborne Field Artillery Regiment within the 82d Airborne Division. This division was one of the elite units, so I was serving with and leading some of the best of the best in the U.S. Army. My position served as the key operational leader and the first officer in the chain of command above the six senior non-commissioned officers (NCOs)—aka chiefs—of the firing battery section. As a recently promoted XO, I found myself in a high-profile position that would reflect highly on my performance evaluations and future command assignments. In other words, it was a position in which I could make an impact.

My predecessor, a West Point graduate, had been relieved for failing to check a critical piece of equipment prior to an airborne operation that highly embarrassed our battalion commander at a division demonstration exercise. They were conducting what is known as a "Drop Zone" mission where artillery pieces are "heavy drop" parachuted in, then airborne personnel jump in and put the howitzers into service after de-rigging to put effective artillery fires down range on a target. The firing block had been left out of one of the howitzers when it was rigged and could not fire a projectile. It would have been a disaster if it were a real-world mission deploying for combat operations.

It was a little awkward stepping into the role because the previous officer was a friend of mine, but I was the senior first lieutenant in the battalion. I had served with my battalion commander after I came back to the United States following a year of service in Korea. I had been assigned to the 82d Airborne Division Artillery (DIVARTY) staff when my commander, a lieutenant colonel, was at the time the executive officer of this brigade-level command. In addition, I had not come up as a second lieutenant in the division like most of my peers, so I was still learning the culture and how to support and be respected by my peers, many whom I was superior to based on my time promoted to first lieutenant earlier than them. Yet I had earned my battalion commander's trust and respect on the division artillery staff, so I found myself assuming a key leadership role.

Develop an Informed Plan of Action

My first major exercise in this new role was leading a brigade-level field training exercise on airmobile transport operations. I had zero experience in this regard other than riding in helicopters during training and as a team leader in Korea and Ranger school. This would be an important exercise for me both in terms of operational proficiency and demonstrating my overall leadership skills.

The exercise would be a "Time on Target" mission that would require us to airlift eighteen 105mm M102 Howitzers and their accompanying soldiers and Humvees to a predetermined location, quickly set them up, and then precisely time the firing of all eighteen of our disparately placed guns so the various shells would land on a single target simultaneously at a predetermined time.

When I received the operations order, I assembled all of our senior non-commissioned officers and section chiefs. We were concerned with how little time we had to prepare before the first CH-47 Chinook helicopter would arrive to transport the howitzers and Humvees. My gunnery sergeant was especially outspoken about his concern since his Humvee would be the first to be picked up and he had no experience rigging the new-model Humvees we'd recently been issued. This was a critical moment; I was the new XO, and he was taking a pretty hard stand. I was sympathetic to his plight, but we had orders and the helicopters were going to arrive whether we liked the time schedule or not. I told him to move out and get the vehicle rigged and ready for transport.

Once he left, I turned my attention to the other non-commissioned officers to plan the balance of the timing since we had to maintain artillery fire support during the battery airmobile movement. I pulled some 3x5" note cards out of my map case and reviewed aloud when each pair of helicopters was scheduled to arrive. I knew we needed to move two howitzers and two Humvees with two CH-47 Chinook choppers per lift, but I wasn't sure about the best process. So I asked for feedback and ideas.

I don't think they were accustomed to this participative leadership style, but they put forth their ideas. I deferred heavily to the thoughts and opinions of my first sergeant who had the most experience amongst us all. Together, we quickly figured out how much time we thought it would take to rig each new Humvee and howitzer for airlift, how many minutes they'd have to pull off the firing line to prepare for the airlift, and how we'd maintain firing capability throughout.

I wrote out 3x5" cards with key time elements for each NCO and gave them their marching orders. When I briefed both the battery commander and fire direction officer, they surprisingly gave me full latitude for my plan.

When the first helicopters arrived, the gunnery sergeant's Humvee was the first to be picked up, as planned. It was rigged, but I noticed when the Humvee got in the air that part of the canvas top was flapping in the wind where it shouldn't have been. Otherwise, things were going fairly smoothly except that the turnaround times between each airlift were slower than anticipated, forcing us to adjust on the fly. I updated the section chiefs and they adjusted their 3x5" cards accordingly.

The cumulative effect of all this was that the Chinooks had to pull off and refuel before my vehicle could be airlifted. I drove to catch up with the rest of the firing battery and arrived at the firing position just shortly before the scheduled target fire mission. The battalion commander was a little frustrated that my Humvee didn't make it on time via airmobile, but at least the fire mission was executed as planned and on time. It was a beautiful sound—all the various howitzers firing off at slightly different times but then hearing one single repercussion as the target down range was hit simultaneously. It was a well-executed, complex mission.

The next morning the first sergeant pulled me aside to pay me one of the highest compliments I'd ever received up to that point in the Army. He told me that our battery airmobile operation was the best executed he'd ever seen in all his years and complimented me on how I led the NCOs and considered their input to formulate a solid plan. It was an important and affirming lesson that served me well the remainder of my time in the Army, as well as in the corporate world and beyond: our best decisions are often not made on our own.

Our best decisions are often not made on our own.

Rather, our best decisions are often made with others who can offer different views and perspectives. Not every decision needs to offer shared ownership or assigned key roles like my particular example, but the input from others we know and trust can generally help us make wise choices.

Whose advice and counsel do you seek when considering a significant decision? Who do you allow to speak into your life? These people are often the inner circle who hold significance in how you approach your life. It is important to have people who help you grow and are affirming in these roles. If they are not, you may want to reconsider how much time you spend with them or how much they may be influencing you without your complete awareness.

Learn from Your Mistakes

During another evaluation exercise, two UH-60 Blackhawk helicopters were to fly two M102 Howitzers forward to a position while the remaining battery continued to provide fire support. The helicopters would then return to pick us up and take us to the main firing battery.

That day we made a successful first-round direct hit, fired our "fire for effect" rounds, and called the choppers back to pick us up. The chief of firing battery from the other unit evaluating us later told me that it had been the best-executed two-gun raid he'd ever seen. It was testimony to the many rehearsals my men had begrudgingly performed in the past, which enabled us to get it down to an art and work as a highly proficient team.

This came about over time, learning from prior mistakes. I always performed an after action review (AAR) and listened to the suggestions of my chiefs and the fire direction team on how we could improve. My section chiefs— experts at what they did—always complained about rehearsing prior to the missions. But because of the continual practice, our battery became the best in airmobile operations and held the second-best "Drop Zone" mission evaluation of the nine artillery batteries in the 82nd Airborne Division that year.

These weren't specific goals of mine when I was thrust into my role but were the result of learning and constantly improving the execution of highly complex missions with lots of moving parts and personalities. My desire from the start was to be the best XO I could be for my artillerymen, for my NCOs, and all those we supported since lives would be in the balance when called to active combat zones. I had to visualize how I would lead these types of missions if given less than eighteen hours to prepare for a hot spot mission with my fellow soldiers.

What are you visualizing? Are you preparing and rehearsing for your goals? Are you learning from your mistakes and improving upon what you're doing? If not, I encourage you to consider performing after action reviews of your own and engaging your inner circle.

I've learned to let others who are affected by my decisions have as much input into the situation as possible. Oftentimes, I've found that they improve upon my ideas because they are closer to the problem or what is needed to implement a change than I am.

Involving others also fosters greater trust. Even if there isn't total agreement on an idea, there is greater ownership in moving forward as a team.

This is true in business, in families, and in relationships. Getting input and advice from those whom you respect, whose counsel you seek, and those whom you love will often lead to better decisions than trying to figure out and implement things on your own.

MARIA'S VIEW

I have a confession to make: Sometimes I struggle to know what direction to take or what I'm supposed to do. Over the years, I began to notice I wasn't the only one who struggled in this area. How *do* you decide what is the next right step? And what happens if you make a mistake?

As I thought and prayed and read about those things, I came up with something that I call "PAAT," which has been a game changer for my discernment and decision making. It was something I personally used but had never shared with others until I was asked to speak at a women's event on the topic of—you guessed it—discernment and decision making. From then on, I have been sharing my little acronym, PAAT.

P=PRAY!
Prayer is always my first building block because I want my life to glorify God; everything I do stems from my love of Him and those around me. I pray about the decision and then I write out the pros and cons and think about them, inviting Jesus into the decision making with me.

A=ASK!
I ask for feedback from one or two trusted people in my life; people I respect and who regularly offer solid wisdom. I limit myself to two people because too many opinions can lead to confusion. I ask the members of this inner circle questions: Do you see anything positive or negative about the choice I'm leaning towards? Am I overlooking anything in my decision making?

It's important to note I don't ask them to tell me what to do; I need to make the final decision and step into the consequences (good or bad!) of my choices.

A=ACT!

It's amazing how I used to stay paralyzed in indecision. I've since discovered that taking action builds momentum. I came to understand I'd never know if something is the right or wrong choice if I didn't make a move. I don't know about you, but in my life, God has never had any problems *closing* doors when they need to be … but even God can't steer a parked car. I've heard many people ask God to open doors and then watch them sit back and wait without doing anything and then get frustrated with the Father for not answering their prayers.

A well-known story that illustrates this mindset is the one in which there was a flood and everyone in the neighborhood decided to evacuate except one man we'll call "Joe." His neighbors pulled their car up to his curb and asked if he wanted to come with them. "Nope, I'm staying here! God is going to save me!" And the neighbors, shaking their heads, drove away.

It rained and rained and as the water rose, Joe first moved up to the second floor, and then onto the roof. As he sat there, a man in a boat came by. "Hey! Do you want a ride?" "Nah!" Joe replied, "God's going to save me!" "Okay," said the man in the boat as he rowed away.

A little while later, when the water was so high Joe was in danger of being swept away, a helicopter arrived and men dropped a rope down to him. "Hey! Grab the rope; we got you!" they shouted. Joe pushed the rope away. "No thanks! I'm good! God is going to save me!" The guys in the helicopter shook their heads, pulled up the rope, and left. A few moments later, Joe was indeed swept away by the rushing waters and died.

When he got to the pearly gates and met Jesus, Joe said to Him, "What gives? I trusted you! But you didn't save me!" Jesus, shaking his head, said, "Joe! I sent you a car, a boat, and a helicopter! What more did you want?"

The moral of the story? God does provide, but we must do our part!

T=TRUST!

Trust; "Let go and let God." My grandma had that little saying hanging on the wall of her house. After I have clarified what I am doing and take action, then I have to trust God that He will take care of me no matter what and trust myself that I can make good decisions. With His help, I can bounce back even when I haven't made a great decision. I can confidently keep moving forward.

I used the PAAT system a few years ago when I was facing a big decision. My lease was up, my work was now fully mobile, and I could finally relocate. But I was on the fence about where to go.

I had always wanted to live by the ocean; nature always makes me feel alive and few things beat a beautiful sunrise or sunset over the water. I had even written my dream down on my goal list and told many people over the previous ten years, "I will live by the ocean; either Florida or one of the Carolinas!" I was convinced I was going to do it.

Finally there were some things that shifted in my life and I realized it was time to take action. But which state should I choose?

I wrote out the pros and cons of each, prayed, and asked for some feedback. North Carolina was the most uncomfortable choice for me as I really only knew two people in the specific city I was considering moving to. I hadn't spent much time there, nor did I have family nearby. Florida was comfortable and familiar to me. It was close to family, one of my best friends lived there, and in many ways, it made sense.

However, as I went through the PAAT process , I came to realize that North Carolina was the right choice. Sometimes, it's the choice that seems to make the least sense and the one that's the most uncomfortable that is the right choice.

Your Words Have Power!

I had the greatest joy of living with three of my dearest and closest friends in Nashville for several years. During our time together, there were many moments when one of us would lament over the way we looked, or did something incorrectly, or handled a situation with a boy. When one of us began to speak negatively about ourselves, the others reminded her that our words have power and then have her repeat an opposite affirmation ten times.

For example, if one of us said, "Gosh, I look terrible today!" she would then be prompted to say, "I look amazing!" or "I am beautiful today!" ten times. We constantly called out the good, true, and beautiful in each other. People are always tearing others down, but when we call out the good, it positively changes the whole atmosphere.

Another example of how the words we speak to ourselves affect our actions is when I was a swim instructor. I taught swimming lessons for a long time and one of the things I would never let my students say was, "This is too hard!"

Growing up, whenever I heard someone say that something was going to be hard to do, I found myself anticipating the negative and dreading an impending struggle. So eventually I decided not to receive the negativity and instead embraced the mindset of it being a good challenge. That tiny change was literally a game changer for me.

So when I heard my swim students say something I asked them to do was too hard, I would smile and tell them, "In Miss Maria's class, no one's allowed to say, "This is too hard." Instead, we say, "This is a *good* challenge and I will do my best!" Every summer, that was my mantra with my kids and they learned it well. It was the coolest thing to watch their actions follow their changed mindset. Suddenly they would eagerly try that new thing and truly believe they could succeed. Often, they did!

Some years later, I received a text message from the mom of one of my students that contained a picture of her daughter's school assignment. When asked to share something that the student had learned from someone that made a difference in her life, she had written, "My swim teacher, Miss Maria taught me 'things aren't hard, they're just a good challenge!'"

And it's true. Nothing is hard unless we make it hard. Life is just full of good challenges!

Learning to Laugh in the Unexpected

In preparation for a women's ministry event that my best friends Christine, Kara, and I were hosting, we created an itinerary that built upon our respective speeches and the songs we would sing together. At the last minute, however, Kara wasn't able to go, which meant Christine and I had to completely revise our talks.

For me, writing a talk takes time, thinking, planning, praying, and contemplating in order to include stories as well as little nuances to help my audience remember whatever it is I'm trying to get across. But with this last-minute shift, I realized I was really going to need to pivot quickly. Internally, I was freaking out but trying to appear calm externally.

The topic I was supposed to dive into was how to walk through a season of suffering. It was during the brief moments before I was to go on stage that the acronym PTSD popped in my head: Praise and thanks, Take thoughts captive, Serve, and Dream.

Why those particular things?

Praise and thanks:

I vividly remember the day I learned this lesson while driving in a rainstorm with equal torrents of tears streaming down my face. I was heartbroken about a situation with a guy, struggling through some painful things within my family, and experiencing lots of challenges at work. As I thought of all the things going wrong in my life and feeling super sorry for myself, I felt the Lord say, "Maria, praise and thank me for this."

Tears welled up even more in my eyes as I said out loud, "Jesus, I can't! There is nothing good about these situations!"

Again, I felt him say, "Maria, thank me for this!" and again I said, "Jesus, I can't!"

My sweet, patient Lord persisted. "Maria, thank me for the rain then because it will help to water the flowers and make them grow and you love their beauty."

"Okay, fine! Thank you, Jesus, for the rain because it makes the flowers grow!"

"Now thank me for your car and being able to drive."

"Thank you Jesus that I can drive and that I have a car…."

For the next twenty minutes or so, Jesus and I went through a million different "thank you and praise you" scenarios until finally I was even thanking Him for the challenging, painful situations I was upset with at the beginning. But the coolest thing? I could feel my emotions completely shift.

Before I knew it, I wasn't feeling so bad, life wasn't terrible, and there actually were a lot of beautiful things going on in my life. It just took focusing on gratitude to get my mind to shift and then, in turn, my emotions. We can't hold gratitude and anxiety at the same time in our brains; literally one will cut off the other. What we focus on expands!

Take your thoughts captive:

There is a reason scripture says to take our thoughts captive. If we let our thoughts just take over, very often we tend to focus on sad and scarce things or painful and negative things. So when we are in a season (or a moment) of suffering, it's important to take such thoughts captive, send them to the cross, ask the Holy Spirit to come fill up that space in our minds, and then choose a new thought that will bear life-giving fruit.

Our thoughts lead us down a journey as you have heard us talk about in this book; our thoughts impact the emotions we experience in our bodies, which then affects our actions, which in turn creates good or bad fruit in our lives. So being super aware of the thoughts we allow to hang out in our minds is imperative!

Serve:

When we are anxious or in a sad place, we tend to withdraw inward and become super self-focused. When we are really self-focused, that usually leads to selfishness and we know that selfishness doesn't bring joy. But if we can think beyond ourselves and go help someone else, or serve those around us, it can release oxytocin which is a feel-good bonding hormone that makes life feel better. In other words, helping others helps you, too! How cool is that?

Dream:

Dreaming (aka creating a new vision) is so important in order to move forward. If we keep replaying the past in our minds—the past sadness, hurt, pain—we will end up repeating it because of our reticular activating system (RAS). We have that beautiful RAS in our brains to help us weed out what we are not focusing on. If we don't give it clear instructions, then we neglect an amazing God-given tool that can help us reach our goals. Our thoughts are literally our greatest God-given superpower … or the most horrific deathtrap. For our thoughts to be our superpower, we must clarify where our focus needs to be!

Remember, what we focus on expands, so choose a new mental picture that is life-giving and can bring some hope.

Your Environment Affects You

Clarifying your inner circle is so important because it enables you to get clear on where you are going, who you want with you on that journey, and what is the next right step. Your habits, beliefs, health, lifestyles, and even your income are dramatically influenced by your social network.

Consider the marine iguanas, native to the Galapagos Islands. Unlike other iguanas, their bodies have literally adapted to find food in their marine environment. Different from the usual green iguana that most of us know, they can remain underwater for up to 30 minutes and even dive up to 100 feet.

Over time, these animals developed blunt noses in order to eat seaweed in tight underwater cracks, webbed feet for swimming, onger claws for clutching slippery rocks, and flat tails that can propel them quickly in the ocean. Even their skin has adapted and is darker to absorb heat from the sun so they remain warm while submerged. Literally every part of their environment shaped their physical bodies.

What's interesting is that we humans aren't much different. According to various research and studies, our environments also play a huge role in shaping us—physically and physiologically. [14] So often, we try to make changes in our lives while ignoring the power that our environments have on us. We believe we can simply use willpower to fight for the changes we desire.

We now know that willpower is not an effective strategy for change. If we want to develop certain habits, the best way is to regularly spend time with the people who have those habits we want.

Benjamin Hardy, who is an organizational psychologist and spent most of his time in grad school studying willpower, argues that people should use their limited willpower to consciously design their environments to make their goals easier to achieve.

Scripture says that, "The one who walks with the wise will become wise, but a companion of fools suffers harm." [15]

Moral of the story? Your inner circle will mobilize you towards actionable behavior. If you don't know what to focus on and there's no clarity, your brain can't help you. What you think about will affect your decisions and shape your life and who you surround yourself with impacts what you're talking about, thinking about, and focusing on.

So choose wisely, my friends!

---

14. The Equality of Opportunity Project, *The New England Journal of Medicine* as well as Harvard and Yale alums James Fowler's and Nicolas Christakis's book, *Connected*, explains how various research on how social networks influence many things in our lives.

15. Proverbs 13:20

JOURNAL EXERCISES

Are you struggling with a decision? Complete the PAAT process:

What will you pray for?

_____

_____

_____

_____

What you will ask for?

_____

_____

_____

_____

How can you take action now?

_____

_____

_____

_____

What will you trust God to do?

_____

_____

_____

_____

Are you sad or depressed? Consider the PTSD actions:

What small things can you praise God or thank Jesus for right now?

_____

_____

_____

What thoughts do you need to take captive and replace?

_____

_____

_____

Whom can you serve in the midst of your struggle?

_____

_____

_____

What future dream can you focus on? Write out your dream in the present text with gratitude: "Thank you Jesus! I am so happy and grateful now that I am……" *(To help you achieve your goal, create a vision board!)*

_____

_____

_____

Develop an Inner Circle:

What trusted friend or family member can help you clarify your goals?

_____

Who can be an accountability partner in your personal or work life?

_____

_____

Is there a coach or guide who can help you refine your dreams into goals and action plans?

_____

_____

Who are the five people you spend the most time with?

1. _____

2. _____

3. _____

4. _____

5. _____

Who are the five people who have the most influence on you in your life? (*Are the five you've noted above the ones you want speaking into your life or do you need to consider modifying who is influencing you?*)

1. _____

2. _____

3. _____

4. _____

5. _____

CHAPTER 7

"Therefore I tell you, whatever you ask in prayer, believe that you have received it, and it will be yours." —Mark 11:24

"You have brains in your head. You have feet in your shoes. You can steer yourself any direction you choose." —Dr. Seuss

---

Thoughts are key. Think it. Create it.

TIM'S VIEW

August 15th, 2015—the day of two life-changing decisions for me.

The first decision was essentially made for me and wasn't the choice I wanted. Though it wasn't unexpected, it was still hard to come to grips with the fact that after twenty-nine years of marriage, it was coming to an end. I had been preparing my sons in conversations, anticipating a divorce. I made sure that I took responsibility for my shortcomings; they needed to hear that from me. Nevertheless, it's humbling and embarrassing to have to explain your failures to others.

The second decision was made by me. I had been wanting to invest in real estate for many years, but this was not supported by my spouse. Now free to make independent decisions, I enrolled in a real estate course and began speaking with real estate investors, like the friend of my CPA who leveraged the resources of other investors to acquire and renovate homes.

He shared his approach, the common challenges, and the successes he was experiencing. Armed with this information, I went all in. I cashed out a 401(k) retirement plan, took the early withdrawal penalty hits from the IRS, and bet on *me*.

As a "hard money lender," I was able to learn about acquisitions and renovations without taking on the risk of doing the renovations myself, even though I was capable of doing them. In each home my wife and I had owned, I had made additions and renovations that always passed code. In fact, a building inspector in Memphis, Tennessee said that my carpentry was better than most of the professionals he inspected on a daily basis.

In any case, investing gave me a clear idea up front of what my return on investment would be and a pretty clear picture of when I would be in a position to reinvest in another project. This enabled me to begin to flip a home with a friend in Seattle, Washington while focusing on my new profession as a real estate agent in Wilmington, North Carolina.

You, too, have the power to create the life you want. Any great accomplishment in business or life first begins with a thought and is followed by emotional highs and lows, challenges and successes.

When you have something on your mind that generates negative thoughts and feelings within you, has anyone ever recommended that you just not think about it? It's not quite that simple, is it? But you can shift your focus by replacing an unhealthy or toxic thought with a healthy one. If you worry about something, you are merely giving it more energy and allowing it to enter your experience. However, if you focus on a positive outcome, you will draw *that* into your life.

It has been said that each of us is like a magnet—whether we consciously realize it or not, we continually attract what we think about. The key, therefore, is to focus our thoughts towards the positive outcomes we desire. We need to hold these thoughts captive and actively pursue our goals.

This book you are reading began as a thought. The excitement I felt when it was first conceived gave life to it. I was encouraged by the thought that writing a book could help others improve their own lives; it was motivation to get started. I began to feel a sense of responsibility to translate my ideas well as I went through the process of formulating an idea, developing an outline, and then writing.

That sense of responsibility led me to ask others for help, get a willing collaborator, and seek the guidance of my inner circle. All of this inspired me to keep going. The same can be true for you, as well.

A Change in Thinking about the Past

I was having breakfast with a friend when she mentioned that her son was going to circumnavigate the earth in commemoration of the 500th anniversary of Magellan's voyage. She was disheartened about not being able to go to Portugal to see him off and was concerned about him and his small crew sailing on the vast ocean in an experimental craft. Ultimately, she had to place her trust in God for his well-being and let go of the idea of personally being there for him.

As she spoke, a strange sensation came over me and a new revelation was given to me. I refer to this as a Holy Spirit moment. I've since had other, similar experiences. It's like I receive a download of new information or a new perspective completely from outside myself. I felt tears welling up in my eyes and in an instant, the guilt and shame I'd carried for nearly forty years evaporated from this new thought: I was going to get to meet my child one day; the one I had never known. I was filled with the joyful anticipation of meeting this person when I get to heaven.

This was a radical departure from how I'd carried the abortion with me all those years. I risked sharing with my friend what had just happened and revealed the truth about my past. It was a powerfully liberating moment.

I'm not saying what happened when I was nineteen years old is acceptable. On the contrary, I still believe the abortion should not have occurred. But I was suddenly liberated from the mental bondage I had been in.

In the book *Today I Begin A New Life*, author Dave Blanchard equates the pain of anguish, shame, and regret with that of spiked metal orbs being pushed into our chests. According to him, in order for us to be able to use our past challenges and unique life experiences for the betterment of others in similar situations, we must first fully embrace our own wounded spaces.

Someone else who had a similar experience was a musician friend of Maria's. He chose to believe strongly that his unborn aborted baby would've been a daughter and that it was her prayers that saved him from a poor life choice. Maria wrote this for him about his daughter he never met.

"Chiara"

You never saw the sun
You never felt the rain
You never knew the air that I breathe
You never got to run
You never got to play
You never got to see what I see

Oh, Chiara Chiara
Angel of mine
Come fly

Beauty like a rose
Eyes of love
I can see you in my mind
Though I never got to hold you
'Cause you were gone
In some way you saved my life

Oh, Chiara Chiara
Angel of mine
Come fly

Oh, Chiara Chiara
Angel of mine
You gave your life

So I might, might fly

Oh Chiara Chiara
Angel of mine
Let's fly

By Maria Spears Copyright 2000 M & M Melodies

Once we've fully accepted the past and recognize similar suffering in others, we can boldly step forward and share our stories to help them. That's what this book is all about. It is our hope that our stories resonate with you and offer you not only hope for a better future, but also tangible action steps to help you begin to make your goal(s) a reality today.

A Way to Test Your Thoughts

The thoughts we think determine the direction of our lives. We have thousands of thoughts every day. Every hour. Every minute. It can be overwhelming if we don't take our thoughts captive. One affirmation I have developed for myself is "I Am a Thought Captor."

It would be ideal if all our thoughts were good and lifegiving, but many times the thoughts in our minds are negative or even toxic. Fortunately, the Bible is a guide to help us test our thoughts. Philippians 4:8 tells us to think about things that are true, noble, right, pure, lovely, admirable, excellent, and worthy of praise. Let's consider each of these thought types:

True

Are we focusing on thoughts that are based on facts or on the opinions of others, including our own perceptions? It's important to focus on what is real, genuine, and authentic: God's word, which provides us with clarity and truth for our daily lives.

Noble

As believers, we are chosen children of God! As such, our thoughts should be elevated and reverently focused on Him, not judging ourselves and others.

Right

This simply means loving what is right and just, and doing what is right because it is the proper thing to do. In order to do the right thing in all circumstances, you must think about what is in fact the right thing to do based on your belief system. Our values and faith guide us.

Pure

For us to be pure in thought we must think of those things that are true, good, and noble, such as protecting another's life or showing compassion towards someone who is suffering.

Lovely

Thinking lovely thoughts means to not only see the goodness and beauty in life, but to also allow our minds to reflect upon those things.

Admirable

Admirable thoughts cause us to think upon things that are commendable and of service to others.

Excellent

When our thoughts are excellent, they are superb, exceptional, and fabulous. The best of the best. Excellent thoughts lead us to live excellent lives.

Worthy of Praise

Thoughts about God—His ways, His plans, and His creation, to name a few—are worthy of praise. It's safe to say that when our thoughts are on Him, that's a good thing.

As we test our thoughts every day, we can use the above as a yardstick to see how well we are capturing our thoughts and recalibrating when needed.

We will never be able to adjust every negative thought that approaches our awareness, but we can certainly try to free our minds from toxic thinking, one thought at a time.

Here's an exercise to help you further reflect upon these ideas: Write out Philippians 4:8 in three different Bible versions. Then compare them, asking God for insight as to how you can turn them into daily habits.

Take Your Thoughts Captive

When you become aware of your thoughts, you have the ability to take them captive. You do not have to believe everything you think, your thoughts are optional. If you are unaware of what you're thinking, then all kinds of old patterns, thoughts, and external circumstances can continue to rule your life. Thought patterns of worrying, worthlessness, fear, or other negative, ingrained thoughts don't serve you well. They become like ruts in the road that we can't get out of.

Sometimes you may not know how or why you got to a challenging place, only that you're in it and you're not certain how to break loose of the situation. Shifting your mindset to healthier thoughts is a good place to start.

You must be intentional about developing this skill. It takes work to control what and how you think. Scripture implores us to take captive our thoughts. This is a skill that takes time to develop. Awareness of the thoughts we are having is the first key step to making conscious choices. From this place of power, you can decide how you want to feel and where you want to spend your energy and time.

When you become aware of unhealthy thoughts, challenge them! Evaluate them. Make choices about them. Ask yourself: Is this thought really true? Am I making a conscious choice or just repeating a pattern?

When you separate yourself from the thought, it loses its power over you. Detach yourself from the thought by writing it out in a journal, stating it out loud, and observing it objectively.

By changing your thinking to an active mindset instead of a passive mindset, you'll start to rewire your brain. Controlling your thoughts will become a skill.

When you are aware of how you think, you have a choice in how you think. Choose wisely.

MARIA'S VIEW

I went on a mission trip to Jamaica the winter after my college graduation. The group I was with didn't build houses or assist with medical care; rather, we simply brought Jesus to people. We spread His love by being His heart, His hands, His voice, and His touch to each person we encountered.

During one particular home visit, I was struck by the level of poverty. The house didn't have a roof and contained dirt floors; there were three-and-a-half walls and there was barely any difference between the inside of it and the outside except for a small fire pit that denoted the "kitchen."

As we approached, we noted an elderly man squatting by the fire preparing his dinner. When we called out to him, he stood and walked towards us. It was then that I realized he was blind.

"How are you?" we asked. A big smile spread across his face as he responded, "I am so good! The Lord's been good to me! The Lord's been so good to me!"

I looked around at what could barely be called a house and tears started streaming down my face. This sweet precious man—blind, no shoes, clothes ragged, his home with a dirt floor and no ceiling—was absolutely certain that "God was so good!" to him. Where was my gratitude? What could I offer to a man who had more joy and gratitude in his pinky finger than I had in my whole body? Very little, I realized.

Yet the smallest thing—a visit—was a reflection of Jesus that brought him much joy. His gratitude was transformational for me. I could bring Jesus to him and others; I could bring them His love. With that in mind, I went back to the place where we were staying, sat down with my guitar, and let the words for a new song pour out: "Lord send me your love...let me be your touch...."

When we feel like we have nothing to offer those around us, we need to remember that we can actually give them the greatest gift of all—Jesus in us. By sharing His love and His touch, we become love incarnate to those around us. That changes people, situations, and the world.

Taking Control of My Thoughts

I love the water; swimming is one of my favorite ways to workout. Growing up, I swam on the swim team and for many years, I was a lifeguard and swim instructor at a local pool. Several summers ago, I began swimming at the YMCA in the early mornings. Every time I was about to get in, I would first stand on the edge and think about how cold the water was going to be, dreading the moment of contact. But then after I dove in, I quickly settled into a rhythm and realized the temperature wasn't that bad! Thinking about how cold it was going to be made it way worse than the actual reality. That's just one example of how our minds can make things out to be worse than they actually are. Our thoughts truly have the power to make us miserable or happy about (or, at the very least, not hate) our circumstances.

Recently I read a book about the science of sound and learned that every cell in our body has a vibrational frequency. In other words, our bodies are made up of different vibrational frequencies (i.e., sounds)! We each comprise a unique symphony; everyone has a specific story that can only be told by them and no one else.

Similarly, as a musician, my instrument is my baby and not just anyone is allowed to play it. When I'm waiting for a gig, I don't let it out of my sight. The same is true of us. As instruments of the Lord, we are so loved and cared for that beautiful music can be played through us. And just as importantly, we are an integral part of a larger symphony; without each one of us, the symphony isn't complete.

Knowing our God-given mission and unique call is a game changer in the way we live our lives. It offers us space to color outside the lines and truly live life by design rather than default.

Remember that every great invention first began as a thought. Someone believed it was possible and asked themselves the necessary "what if" questions. In order to create, you have to think. Daily "thinking time" can be a powerful way to let your mind relax and help you make wise decisions.

Live life by design rather than default.

Yet many of us, when we have a free moment, grab our phones out of habit. We are so used to being continuously stimulated that the mere thought of not having anything to do for a few moments makes us uncomfortable. However, it's that down time that can be most powerful for thinking through things and creating something amazing, like a book or a new business idea or solving a problem in your life.

This intentional thinking time is a key skill for greater self-awareness. It is also a critical skill for renewing your mind and moving your thoughts towards becoming the person you intend to be. The skill of conducting a "thought recon" is useful to begin the process of changing the underlying circumstances that are negatively shaping your thoughts and emotions, enabling you to move in the direction you want to go.

JOURNAL EXERCISES

What thoughts are you thinking right now?

_____

_____

_____

_____

_____

Are your current thoughts motivating and moving you towards your life goals? If not, what can you think today to begin the process of change you want for yourself?

_____

_____

_____

_____

_____

Do you have a coach? A guide? A mentor? Who are you going to enlist to help you start to make these changes in your life?

_____

_____

_____

_____

_____

CHAPTER 8

"For I know the plans I have for you", declares the Lord, "plans to prosper you and not to harm you, plans to give you hope and a future". —Jeremiah 29:11

"The instant you accept responsibility for everything in your life is the moment you acquire the power to change it." —Ed Mylett

---

REFLECT The Life You Want™

By now you've taken the time to complete the exercises at the end of each chapter, which has provided you with a roadmap to create the life you want.

To recap, REFLECT represents:

R=Recognize You've realized that you can change your life. You are not a victim; you are the creator of your life experience.

E=Each Day Hopefully, you've begun the practice of reflecting on what you are grateful for each day. We encourage you to make this a daily practice going forward for the rest of your life. Consider using the REFLECT The Life You Want™ Journal or the exercises at the end of each chapter as a daily resource.

F=Feel A feeling of happiness emerges as you focus on and begin to overcome challenges, achieve goals, and experience the state of being that you've laid out for yourself. Use your imagination.

L=Love Keep finding ways to love yourself and to share your love with others. If you've found this book helpful, please share it with others. Give a copy to someone you love as an expression of your love for them. They'll be grateful that you did.

E=Energize Stay energized with thoughts that keep yourself moving forward. If you have setbacks, shift your focus back to the life you intend to create for yourself. Keep the positive emotions and thoughts flowing. If you can change your mindset, it will transform your life!

C=Clarify Who is speaking into your life? Do you surround yourself with people who are elevating you? What do you listen to? Read? Engage regularly with your inner circle and consider hiring a coach to help you clarify how to achieve your dreams and keep you accountable as you move towards them.

T=Thoughts Your thoughts are key to creating a mindset that supports who you want to become. Remember the most important principle of human life: You become what you think about. Your outer world is always going to be a reflection of your inner world.

It's up to you. So be confident, take action, and REFLECT The Life You Want™!

COACHING

As co-authors, we encourage you to seek a guide to help you develop a greater mindset and skill sets to achieve your dreams. A guide, or coach, can help you see your thought patterns and help you clarify your thoughts in to grow new skills. Focus on rewiring your subconscious mind—the 95% you are not normally using in your day-to-day activities.

If you'd like help with your mirror care, we would love to assist you. As coaches, we guide you throughthe process of dream expansion—moving from what you believe to be possible, to stretch goals, to what seem like impossible goals. We help you develop your dream skill set and learn how to dream effectively through assessments, exploring your desires, and developing new skill sets.

Contact us to schedule a consultation and listen to our respective podcasts for weekly mindset mastery tips to help you REFLECT The Life You Want™.

Tim Howard

www.themirrorbook.com

Tim@TheMirrorBook.com

REFELCT The Life You Want™ Podcast

Maria Spears

www.mariaspears.com

mariaspears3@gmail.com

Girl, Water Your Grass! Podcast

We are grateful and happy that you have taken the time to read *The Mirror: 7 Steps to Reflect The Life You Want*™. If you purchased this book, thank you. If it was given to you as a gift, thank the person who gave it to you. If you enjoyed it, consider buying a copy for a friend and leaving a 5-Star review for us at Amazon.com.

CHAPTER 9

"As water reflects the face, so one's life reflects the heart" —Proverbs 27:19

"I am not what I think I am, and I am not what you think I am, I am what I think you think I am" —Charles Horton Cooley

Mirror Care

When I came across this sticker on the back of a mirror as I began to write this book, I was struck by how analogous the instructions on how to remove the label, hang the mirror, and clean the face of the mirror were to our lives.

When we are birthed into this world, we are covered with blood and amniotic fluid. Nurses gently wash us off and wrap us in a clean, fresh cloth. Much like the mirror, great care is used during this process so as to not harm us.

Like hanging a mirror, our parents carefully bring us up in a good environment, with values that will help us become successful in life. The support and encouragement of family, friends, and teachers—the "hooks and wires," as it were—provide us with the initial support we need as we go forth in life.

As we grow older, we begin to rely upon more people. If we marry, our spouse will become our most important mirror—a treasure who will likely become our clearest mirror if we provide them with proper love and care.

Conversely, we are also a mirror to someone else, reflecting onto them what we see in ourselves. Taking care of ourselves is vital in order to offer a clean, clear reflection to those who look to us for friendship, love, or safety. The "cleaner" our mirror is, the more accurately we are able to reflect something that is life giving.

So let's take care of the "mirrors" in our lives; they help us shift our thoughts towards the right direction to help us reach our goals.

And just as importantly, we need to take care of our mind, body, and soul to be a clear mirror to others.

WHAT NEXT

Now that we've walked through the principles to REFLECT The Life You Want™, you may be wondering, *What should I do next?* That ultimately will be your decision, but if something has resonated within these pages, we encourage you to start there. Start *now*!

Be encouraged by the following poem, written in 1897 by Eleanor Amerman Sutphen and popularized by the famous missionary Elisabeth Elliot (1926–2015) on her radio program, "Gateway to Joy" (emphases added):

From an old English parsonage down by the sea
There came in the twilight a message to me;
Its quaint Saxon legend, deeply engraven,
Hath, it seems to me, teaching from Heaven.
And on through the doors the quiet words ring
Like a low inspiration: *"Do the next thing."*

Many a questioning, many a fear,
Many a doubt, hath its quieting here.
Moment by moment, let down from Heaven,
Time, opportunity, and guidance are given.
Fear not tomorrows, child of the King,
Trust them with Jesus, *do the next thing.*

Do it immediately, do it with prayer;
Do it reliantly, casting all care;
Do it with reverence, tracing His hand
Who placed it before thee with earnest command.
Stayed on Omnipotence, safe 'neath His wing,
Leave all results, *do the next thing.*

Looking for Jesus, ever serener,
Working or suffering, be thy demeanor;
In His dear presence, the rest of His calm,
The light of His countenance be thy psalm,
Strong in His faithfulness, praise and sing.
Then, as He beckons thee, *do the next thing.*

ACKNOWLEDGMENTS

TIM

I'm grateful for my sons, family members, former colleagues, consultants, mentors, leaders, and instructors who have helped to shape my thinking and growth over the years. I'd like to mention a few people in particular who have tremendously impacted the content of this book.

I'm appreciative of Noreen Watson, my learning partner from my Master's program who helped me with so many personal learnings and continued to support and inspire me as a leader after our training. She was my initial collaborator on this project and helped me to clarify my early thinking about what should unfold amongst these pages.

I'm grateful for my friend Royd Lutz, with whom I reconnected as parts of this book were written. It was great to rekindle a friendship and get his invaluable perspective about some of our shared Army Ranger experiences.

I'm grateful for my Master Coach of The Man School, Bill Schnieders, for inspiring me and bringing forth some of the ideas that would encourage and propel me towards my dreams.

I'm especially grateful for my co-author and friend Maria Spears. Sometimes you encounter people for a season so that you may learn from them or so you can help them. They might even become your friends for a period of time and you encourage each other. But then there are those once-in-a-lifetime encounters when someone alters the trajectory of your life forever.

Such is the case when Maria entered my life. I was immediately struck by her presence; I affectionately refer to her as a "room changer." She has been both a catalyst and inspiration for me to learn more and bring more to this manuscript. She is a role model for me and for her other friends and clients. She walks the talk.

We thank our Editor, Dalene Bickel, of Lasting Legacies, who helped Maria and I improve upon our manuscript to become this book you have now had the opportunity to read.

And thank you, dear reader. I am hopeful that you will be inspired by the ideas and exercises within the pages of this book we have shared with you.

Our intention is that you apply these principles into your life in order to transform it so you can fulfill your own unique calling and purpose in life. Remember that you are created for greatness, for wholeness, and for completeness.

MARIA

I'm grateful for all of you who, over the years, have encouraged and asked me to write a book; you guys know who you are. Thank you to my WEST Gals; you ladies level me up in every way and I love you to pieces! "A rising tide raises all ships!"

Thank you also to His Own; you sisters have believed in me and encouraged me and truly been the sisters I never had. "Flowerhouse forever!" So much love!

Thank you to Lauren Blair and Ang Schneiders for being fellow entrepreneurs, growth and faith-minded sisters who I can bounce ideas off of.

Thank you to my Love, Matt; I'm grateful for the ways we've learned and will be forever learning to be a mirror for one another. "Verso l'alto!" You are the kindest thing God has done for me.

Thank you to my parents, Ray and Jeanie, for instilling in me early on a love for God and others, for learning, growth, health and fitness and for encouraging the fearless intentional pursuit of going after what I believe God is calling me to do no matter what.

Thank you to my brothers, Seth, Josh, Adam, David and Joe; you guys have helped form who I am in more ways than you'll ever know and I'm so grateful for each of you and the ways you've pushed and challenged me, loved and encouraged me. Thank you also for marrying such amazing women! Grateful for my 'sisters'!

Thank you to my co-author Tim Howard for your friendship and for inviting me into this project. It's been both a joy and a "good challenge" with so many important lessons learned along the way. I'm grateful for you, our friendship and collaboration.

Thank you to our readers! Truly. Go out there and become even more of who you are!

And last, but not least, thank you sweet Jesus for the gift of this one, beautiful, amazing life and for the tools you have given us all to REFLECT the Life we want! It's all for You.

REFLECT The Life You Want™

WITH TIM HOWARD

Listen to Tim Howard, Host of the 'REFLECT The Life You Want™' Podcast:

GIRL, WATER YOUR GRASS

With Mary Katherine Wathen and Maria Spears

@girlwateryourgrass

Listen to Maria Spears, Co-Host of the 'Girl, Water Your Grass' Podcast

The end goal of
achievement is not
what you get from it,

but who you become
along the way.

To learn more about Coaching with Tim Howard
email: Tim@TheMirrorBook.com

MAXIMUM
POTENTIAL
COACHING

To learn more about
Coaching with Maria Spears
Contact her at: Maria@TheMirrorBook.com